Gift Revisited

Gift Revisited

A Minister's Recovery from Despair!

BILL W. HOLLEY JR.

RESOURCE *Publications* • Eugene, Oregon

GIFT REVISITED
A Minister's Recovery from Despair!

Copyright © 2022 Bill W. Holley Jr. All rights reserved. Except for brief quotations in critical publications or reviews, no part of this book may be reproduced in any manner without prior written permission from the publisher. Write: Permissions, Wipf and Stock Publishers, 199 W. 8th Ave., Suite 3, Eugene, OR 97401.

Resource Publications
An Imprint of Wipf and Stock Publishers
199 W. 8th Ave., Suite 3
Eugene, OR 97401

www.wipfandstock.com

PAPERBACK ISBN: 978-1-6667-5725-5
HARDCOVER ISBN: 978-1-6667-5726-2
EBOOK ISBN: 978-1-6667-5727-9

VERSION NUMBER 121222

The chapters in italics were developed from original sermon manuscripts.

To my loving wife Linda, who has shared in this journey in more ways than anyone will ever know. For more than fifty years her desire for our marriage to have authentic meaning has never been compromised, has never faltered. To her I am eternally grateful for her love and support. Her prayers have kept us both forward-looking. Her incredible skill and understanding of my mind are clearly visible in the conclusion of this book—it is from her "pen" that it is written.

So early in the morning Jacob took the stone that he had put under his head and set it up for a pillar and poured oil on the top of it. He called the name of that place Bethel. But the name of the city was Luz at the first. Then Jacob made a vow, saying, "If God will be with me and will keep me in this way that I go, and will give me bread to eat and clothing to wear, so that I come again to my father's house in peace, then the Lord shall be my God, and this stone, which I have set up for a pillar, shall be God's house. And of all that you give me I will give a full tenth to you."

—Genesis 28:18–22.

God said to Jacob, "Arise, go up to Bethel and dwell there. Make an alter there to the God who appeared to you when you fled from your brother Esau." So, Jacob said to his household and to all who were with him, "put away the foreign gods that are among you and purify yourself and change your garments. Then let us arise and go up to Bethel, so that I may make there an alter to the God who answers me in the day of my distress and has been with me wherever I have gone."

—Genesis 35:1–3

Contents

Introduction | 1

Chapter 1
The Genesis of the Project | 3

Chapter 2
Light Was Breaking | 7

Chapter 3
The Inherent Value of a Revisit | 10

Chapter 4
Enslaved by the Autobiographic | 13

Chapter 5
Deceptions of the Mind | 17

Chapter 6
Inevitability of Distress | 22

Chapter 7
The Need for a Revisit | 25

Chapter 8
Revisit, To What Purpose? | 27

Chapter 9
The Temptation to Give Up on Meaningful Pursuits | 31

Chapter 10
Before You Give Up! | 35

Chapter 11
Substance Revealed | 50

Chapter 12
How to Live Authentically: No Pretense Necessary | 53

Chapter 13
It's Howdy Doody Time | 57

Chapter 14
Knowing and Understanding Yourself | 65

Chapter 15
Treasure Buried Within: A Search for Identity | 70

Chapter 16
The Simple Truth | 89

Chapter 17
Reasoning: Its Influence and Use | 91

Chapter 18
A Godlier Reasoning | 95

Chapter 19
Theodicy: Living Authentically Through Crisis | 98

Chapter 20
Bob Godfrey Died Yesterday | 102

Chapter 21
Reflections from the Past | 113

Chapter 22
The Mystery of Restoration | 117

Chapter 23
Living with the Rights We Have: A Call for Civil Obedience | 120

Chapter 24
What Rights Do We Have? | 129

Chapter 25
Our Search for God | 150

Conclusion
Additional Reflections | 165

Bibliography | 167

Acknowledgements

*I herein recognize my childhood friend
Jack Eades and his wife Vicki.
Not only did God use Jack as a "first inspiration"
but his encouragement and long-suffering in
response to the early rough draft
is deeply appreciated.*

*I want to acknowledge my wife Linda who
painstakingly worked through the first draft
making many helpful suggestions and corrections.
Secondly, I want to acknowledge the excellent
editing work done on the final manuscript by
Reta Beall, Yukon, Oklahoma.*

Introduction

"But this one thing I have against you, you have lost your first love" (Rev 2:4).[1]

ENCASED IN THE FOLLOWING pages are a few forty to fifty-year-old sermon manuscripts—more appropriately defined as essays that address critically important subject matters. They present a discourse on important life themes, teachings around which service to the church is centered. For me, they represent the emotional overflow of a journey back to Bethel—the heightened place of inspiration. Conversely, they identify the place at which the disintegration of my ministry in the church began. For many, the journey can take place, as it did for me, after having survived many years in an often-uninspired existence, a life that was spiritually fractured.

More than anything, my *revisit* to Bethel vividly exposed pride and ego, the burdensome reflections of spiritual distress. The imposing memory was softened by a renewed sense of value that appeared, reminding me of the authentic value my life had been provided. For certain, it was a catharsis, a new freedom, a tomorrow no longer impeded by the burdens with which I had lived for many years.

It can be argued that any value these writings have ends with my attempt to display some ecclesiastical talent. They may or may not represent a convincing level of scholarship, may not even possess any recognizable inspiration. However, I encourage you to examine each as you read. If nothing else, they can serve as a vivid reminder of the standard by which one is called to live. They may even help chart a fresh understanding of your own faith. My rediscovery of the manuscripts brought a reminder of a time

---

1. Unless otherwise noted, all scripture is taken from the English Standard Version of the Bible.

when my faith was real and vibrant. I was amazed with the spiritual exactness and the understanding by which God had, during my early ministry, inspired and blessed me.

There is the possibility you can come to better appreciate the gift of ministry with which you have been provided, especially if some lack of authentic God-honoring leadership has syphoned your enthusiasm and distracted you from its genuine meaning. Regardless of the station in life at which you have come to rest, you may need a sabbatical, a time of reflection, a time of renewal, a repurposing of the gift of service with which God has blessed you. A trip back to Bethel is a possibility for those over whom a cloud of despair has lingered, one that has altered the hope of each day and blighted the promise of every tomorrow. A Bethel experience can have a way of lightening the burdens you carry that have altered your utter dependence on God.

I suppose most who serve in the church have or will have times that prevent an exact focus on the work to which they have been called. It is possible to soften the distress in our lives by reestablishing the points of origin which are to be discovered, not new but with renewed beginnings.

Chapter 1

The Genesis of the Project

THERE ARE TIMES WHEN we suddenly feel we may have reached the end—that life is on a downward trajectory and cannot be calmed or diverted from inevitable disintegration. I was particularly overwhelmed by the feeling one early spring day in 2019. An overgrowth of ugly weeds had for weeks been beckoning me to our small backyard. My wife and I were not completely settled, although we had moved into the house several months earlier. In the downsizing that resulted from an unwanted move, we became aware that the unexpected twists and turns of life, along with evaporating income, whether brought on by aging or unyielding circumstances, can solicit a grey covering of disappointments.

On that spring day, I yielded to an unalluring invitation, but only with a sense of reluctancy. The reasons for my feelings were endless, convictions faint and scattered, and the project of pulling weeds seemed too burdensome for my weary and crippled frame of mind and body. The anticipation of any accomplishments in an allergy-invested backyard, a tangled mess of annoying weeds, seemed not only unpleasant, but unreasonable. The unwanted task held no attraction, short of a nagging guilt that aggravated me.

Nothing regarding the experience appeared rewarding. It is strange how life's redefining, course-altering moments can suddenly drop by unexpectedly to enlighten our private and bewildering universe. Who could have imagined that such unsolicited labor, undertaken only through guilt and disintegrating circumstances, would serve to unmask a fortuitous beacon. Who would have suspected that such a task could direct me to a time and circumstance that not only gave rise to a nostalgic and rewarding journey, but also served to supplant lingering fears and escalating disappointment, yielding to a new and exciting platform for living out the last years of my life? I did not anticipate that pulling weeds would be therapeutic, that the task would suddenly help repair a belabored and wounded spirit. I did not expect it to attract and enhance my understanding of the path and circumstances that had defined my journey, nor did I anticipate that it would expand my perspective on the twists and turns of life to which I seemed to have fallen victim.

It is strange that the decisions we make, the assumptions at which we arrive, the shifts and alterations of the routine, the commonplace can suddenly yield to a hidden and silent voice, contemplative thought dressed in a garment of the ordinary. If we allow them to, self-conceived reflections can help cleanse the fragmented mysteries of life and suddenly yield to an explosive awakening of new possibilities, elevating awareness to recognizable promise. Too often, prayer can be consumed by strange and disingenuous thought, suffocated by melancholy reflection. It is amazing how often contemplative thought can, with alerting intensity, dance across the most stale and insignificant exercises. The manicuring of landscape is no exception.

And then ... the phone rang. I welcomed the distraction. For some reason, my usual reluctance to take calls, in this time of caller ID, was overturned. The incoming call displayed a West Virginia area code, and although I had not lived there for more than fifty years, I answered. The voice at the other end sounded familiar. My momentary caution instantly vanished hearing "This is Jack, your old friend." More than forty years had passed since we had last spoken. Jack and I had been best friends, had grown up together. Early in the conversation, a faint caution lingered, reminding me of a few long-gone moments when envy had made an unwelcomed appearance in our friendship. I felt some element of shame for allowing it, but quickly released the emotion, reminding myself how young children can so easily be tempted to jealous, even disparaging thoughts.

Occasionally, envy can be a good thing. It easily translates into the higher resolve for new, better, loftier goals, a more passionate reach for achievement. I quickly determined that any childish tendency to be jealous was momentary, easily dismissed. I was not overcome by embarrassment or even marginally shamed when I recalled that I, in my struggle for self-value, had on occasion succumbed to misguided envy of Jack, allowing some insecurity to seep into my relationship with him. At its genesis, the writing of this book really was reflective of a self-fulfilling nose-dive into the waters of my limited, even disappointing accomplishments. I simply

The Genesis of the Project

set out to prove that, at last, I had overcome that raw and sensitive nerve of believing I would never amount to much, as my seventh-grade science teacher had voiced with an educational prophecy.

The irony is that my teacher's sharply calibrated evaluation came shortly after the school administration made the decision to pull me, along with Jack and ten or so fellow students, out of the normal classroom setting for a kind of trial experiment. What I, and probably my classmates as well, did not know then was that earlier testing had suggested that we had a leg up on the capacity to excel academically. For sure, I did not think I was all that gifted. It was only years later, after I took a grownup IQ test, that I began to realize and trust my brain power, and I was suddenly justified in challenging the accuracy of that seventh-grade science teacher's forecast.

Jack's call came at a time of genuine bewilderment in my life, a time when any semblance of productivity, any hint of usefulness at a quickening pace had been washed away. The pride and selfcenteredness that had led to my leaving the preaching ministry more than forty years before had forever remained encrypted by various shades of obliqueness. I had buried them deeply yet those painful and haunting memories often flashed with recognizable brilliance.

A few days after the call, for whatever reason, I turned to a manila folder of dusty sermon manuscripts. I had been both surprised but also shamed by Jack's confession when he said, "I have often taken notice of your work, observed at a distance the direction your life has taken. I must say your work has been an inspiration to me. In many ways, I am in ministry today because of your life's work." His words, were shocking and unexpected. What I did not know was that Jack was well into adulthood before making his confession of faith. I was surprised when I learned that his new faith had led him to sell a very successful insurance practice, move away from his luxurious home that he had built on the cliffs of the famous New River Gorge. and head off to seminary with his family.

Talking to Jack left me with a question: What was it about my life, what meager accomplishments did I have that could have helped blaze a trail on which someone, anyone, like Jack could have traveled? Had I been graced with a depth of understanding, one that had vanished when I resigned from my church? Had preaching been the fundamental means through which my faith had been more authentically experienced? I desperately needed answers to my inquiry. Would the exploration of some ancient writings remind me of the sacred ground on which I had once stood? Could I regain in any demonstrative way a fresh and renewed understanding of the truths on which my life had been founded? Would I be granted the opportunity to voice once again the fundamental understandings of my faith, a faith that could encourage a brother or two to alter directions, to reembrace the ministry on to which he (or she) had once so tightly held? I reasoned that a journey back to Bethel might hold some answers.

The plan was simple. I would reproduce a handful of my favorite messages, allowing my journey over the years to find a place in the renewed stories. The outline of the original message would not be altered much. The words and most of the illustrations would remain intact although the length would be stretched. Most of all, my experiences, my flaws, my humanity would not be lost in the jumbled phrases of a desperate, inquisitive mind exploring questions for which no immediate answers existed and for which no one seemed to be searching.

Call these revised writings sermons if you must. I now identify them as essays. I choose rather to see them for what they are, the experience of a *revisit* to the place where God was, more than at any other point in time, infinitely real to me. There is nothing profound about this journey. Some who read this book will feel the warmth of that moment when God was most real to them. We, people of faith, have each had our own times of miracle. Most have been private; only a few have been shared.

Chapter 2

Light Was Breaking

WHEN I DISCOVERED THE dusty sermon manuscripts in an old file drawer, I was, for some reason, compelled to peer into the mirror of my soul, clearly reviewing a kaleidoscope of ascending and descending accomplishments. I recognized that each message had not been designed because of my own industry but because God had graced me with a *gift*. This reasoning eliminated any argument that the writings were the product of my own initiative, the result of my own stimulating and perceptive intellect.

Although the scene was, in so many ways, exhilarating and redeeming, I understood, perhaps for the first time, that the gift of preaching had been entrusted to me, had been on loan to me as a gift of grace. It was also a poignant reminder that my work in the church had been overtly compromised through willful neglect and onerous misuse. I had allowed it to be glazed over because of pride and egocentricity. The exposure to the file of sermons awoke me to the *good* with which I had been entrusted and the *bad* that had soured and blighted my purpose. I recognized the bad remorsefully, an insignia of the ugly memory with which I had silently lived for decades. Most will understand the variety and shapes by which these misappropriations of duty erupt.

I was sadly reminded again that the gift of preaching that I had employed nearly fifty years ago had been withdrawn, stored away in some fortuitus time-capsule, but would now, for an infinitesimally brief time, be again opened. Like glistening jewels, priceless and rare, the sermons appeared, standing in the innocence of their original purpose. The dross of disappointment had been washed away. A clarity, an understanding of my faith, warmly and graciously appeared. Six of those sermons are embedded in this narrative. In them I discovered a surging energy, one that was not then and is not now marginalized or subjugated to some acrobatic sensationalisms.

The writings I am sharing are rewrites. Essays! They reflect my faith and my heart. Just that. Nothing more. I have thoroughly revised some of the sermons although the coloration of the time when they were written remains. I chose to retain the pulpit style and language as originally drafted and footnoted, but I did recognize the need to surrender to a more and updated subject matter. Each of the selected sermons escorted me to a moment of truth, a time when the clammer of the world had not thoroughly and completely suffocated the benefits of a life lived in utter devotion to God. My eyes were opened again to a time during which a godly purpose stood with clarity, a time where grace and resiliency of faith transcended my weaknesses and disparaging tendencies. I again felt God's abiding presence; he was so close that nothing could dissuade or alter the joy preaching provided.

When originally framed, these sermons stood with purity, purpose, and persuasion. When I pondered them, each word released a forgotten reality and reassured me that the sustaining presence of God was fundamentally unshakeable. They revealed again a Lord who knew and understood me in my sinful and elaborately crafted manners of insincerity. More often than we willingly acknowledge, the minister's life, in fact every man's life, can be a series of rejections, heartache and despair, tragedy relentless and seemingly unfair. Conversely, if one is courageous enough to invite joy and purpose into it, life can be an adventure, a canvas on which to capture an utter dependence on God. It can produce the miraculous that can displace the disappointment but can also greatly reduce the jagged and disenfranchising noises of misdirection to which we so frequently succumb.

God allowed my revisit to do that for me. I was guided to a unique moment of conception, a span of time, an unfathomable experience in which my call to ministry had, through the gift of preaching, been fully and completely confirmed. I was overwhelmed by reflections when integrity and the authentic stood exposed with undeniable clarity. For each who dares to risk it, a revisit can provide succinct and profound awareness. It can bring joy and fulfillment strangely back into focus, unencumbered by frustration or bewilderment, and in doing so, it can replenish many of the regrets and disappointments.

For certain, there will be painful moments. They cannot be ignored or misunderstood because of reverberating anger or an unforgiving spirit. A revisit may shame us as it exposes our failure to capture the abundance with which we are daily being graced. It, perhaps more than anything else, can unleash an acknowledgement that life's most promising and fulfilling moments emanate more completely and unyieldingly from a selfless surrender to the divine and unintrusive Lordship of the Christ from Galilee.

Chapter 3

The Inherent Value of a Revisit

ANY VALUE TO BE experienced from this book ultimately will be adjudged by the audience for whom it was written. *Gift Revisited* might portend some value to the clergy in general, but more specifically, it is directed towards church leaders whose own experiences might bear some resemblance to the author's. My heart yearns desperately to know that some struggling brother or sister will discover solitude from this book, taste renewed hope, find comfort, and be encouraged by the Biblical truths passionately examined.

Initially, I assumed that those who might best benefit from this book would hold some leadership position in the church. This group might be identified as *wounded ecclesaholics.* Much like the writer, this group has been bruised by the roller coaster ride that seems inevitable for those called into Kingdom work. Every profession has moments of disdain and failure—times when the spirit is shaken, when shadow and turpitude swell in massive crescendo and plunge each to his times of despair. On these occasions, defeat and failure are so close that the inevitability of destruction joins hands with an ever-expanding naïveté.

Although we clergy-type are to blame for most of our scars and wounds, we still find it difficult to accept that our profession often takes us through valleys and over peaks. We fail to realize that it is often a painful excursion that only a fellow struggler with whom we share similar moccasins can completely understand. *Gift Revisited* acknowledges such an excursion. Some of you might find unexpected value by reading this book.

Your journey, if you dare to take it, will bear little resemblance to mine—your revisit to the time of a transformative faith experience cannot and should not, with any accuracy, attempt to replicate the experiences of my revisit. Only your openness to imagination, to the intruding benevolent presence of the Holy Spirit of God can point you to your own special time and place where truth appears absolute—a sanctuary of comfort where all seems right and inviting—the feeling of being at home with yourself and with God. It can be overwhelming. Your visit may be brief, but it can be life-altering. It can be a journey for new beginnings, a time for renewal, the discovery of a lost hope, and the reward of an enduring promise.

My revisit to the adolescence of faith was not enacted with misrepresentation, nor was it an embarkment crafted to mend broken dreams or the clamoring inventory of a thousand "I wish I had" transactions. I simply shifted my emotional energy from my rapidly eroding, nearly exhausted purpose in life to quietly listen to the genuine heartbeat of some old sermon manuscripts. I began to feel again the good pleasure of a time when closeness to God invited a profound awareness by which to recognize once more the Father's love—joyful, meaningful times that disallowed the infusion of worldly influence and the remorse of burdensome compromise.

Please do not assume that your visit is a caravan marching in retreat to steady the rudderless ships of your discontent. Rather, this "time is like a one-way street that leads . . . to the future and never allows me to turn back to the past stations of my life and make revision. Therefore, I am in the grip of my past and cannot redo it. I am a prisoner of my own past, and that past is dreadfully irreversible."[1] While acknowledging this raw truth, your revisit can still mysteriously invite a renewal of spirit and a replenishing of will. It can produce new focus and design for the future—a consoling awareness that God has never abandoned you, has not stepped away from the moments of clouded and disjointed wandering to which those in ministry are instinctively exposed. It can be risky. It will, of certain, invite recurring confession and may provide only a scant hint of replenished reconciliation, but it will, if you invite the thought, supply the meaningful awareness that God has never stepped aside, has never given up on you. In fact, you may be called to seek an unconditional forgiveness—even given a new assignment. The pleasure of writing this book has, in part, been a reward of my revisit. The experience has brought a reinvigoration of my faith, a refreshing exploration to better understand the God on whom my life has been anchored. The burden of the lost gift to which I had become enslaved has not gone away, but its intrusive and debilitating weight has been lessened.

---

1. Thielicke, *Life Can Begin Again*.

It may perhaps be at this juncture that your story can take on greater significance. I have been provided a fresher parchment on which to design my future, a new lens through which to view my value and a new hope from which more optimism and resourcefulness can come. I can still find value in the reflection of the past, still understand the need for remorsefulness and forgiveness, but I have now found a more productive and rewarding way to map out each day in anticipation of the next.

Chapter 4

Enslaved by the Autobiographic

I HAVE MADE A sincere effort to find some more specific reason why someone might choose to read this book. Perhaps my desire stems from my awareness that a reader might discover some level of kinship with me—reach the place where circumstances and the inevitable displeasures of life might be seen with greater clarity and understanding. I desperately want that to happen.

On more than one occasion, an observer or two have hinted that my purpose for writing is only to have a platform from which I might have my say, a medium that might nourish my lingering, often noticeable, thirst for affirmation. The assumption that my purpose for writing, using my talent for slapping together some marginally inspired yet hopefully brilliant ideas, is a misguided one despite my overbearing tendencies to clamoring rhetoric or my propensity to seldom refrain from voicing everything that comes to mind. Although occasionally guilty of the aforementioned accusation, my purpose for writing is not the product of this painful journalistic assessment. My thesis for this writing extends well beyond.

Gift Revisited may become to my family and friends a more confessional unveiling of my genuine self; hopefully, it is one not blighted by disappointment or by any shades of distain. My family and associates may enjoy wading through my meandering thoughts. They may even discover a larger me, not a different or a more attractive version than they have of me, but one with whom they can identify. They can get to know one who has not only lived in the shadow of his own frailty, but who has also aspired, despite many faulty efforts, to do the right and noble thing. Although this objective was the initiatory cause, the reason soon morphed in anticipation of a broader audience, into a larger, more exact and easily defined group now identified by the sobriquet *ecclesaholics*—some perilously wounded, many obviously anxious and frightened, others selfishly deceived, all hopelessly entangled in kingdom work. I cannot help but wonder if most believers, especially those who have emotionally, maybe even physically, walked away from a vocational ministry, might not find restoration, at least in part, by examining this book. It is a wishful thought.

Ultimately, my readers will determine the influence of the Spirit on the writer, but more importantly, the presence of the Spirit of God in his or her own narrative. Edward William Fudge writes,

> Any child of God can ask assistance in weighing the message of uninspired authors while beseeching a spirt of wisdom and revelation in the knowledge of the things God has said. This not only comforts; it creates a sense of humility and of responsibility. We must open Scripture prayerfully and then handle it with care. We must then listen to it without objection or argument. It is the Word of the living God.[1]

Ultimately, the reader must determine if God's voice is audible to him in this book. Can it also redirect, bringing some level of healing to the discouragement and lessen some, or even most, of the shame with which he may have silently lived for a significant portion of his life?

It is assumed that the major group for which this writing might have potential value, for whom the theological rhetoric might have meaning, are those who have professional engagement in the work of the church. Church leaders and students of the scripture are more likely to find an idea, even insights from which they might further expand understanding of themselves. We can, if we try, learn an occasional thing or two from a wandering mind. Theological training and professional experience alone may not fully qualify me to make these observations, but life experiences do.

As I have, for several months now, applied not-so-nimble fingers to the keys of my laptop, much soul-searching has overshadowed my original thinking. It is not that I have wandered mindlessly in search of imaginary success and egocentric value. Daily petition has been offered to ward off such potentially destructive influence. Much to my surprise, humility has not been totally ignored or out of reach. I have come to believe that the direction this writing has taken me has gathered not only creative momentum but that it has also brought some clarity to my own soul. I now think

---

1. Fudge, *The Fire That Consumes*, 22.

that this book can have significant value for most who might choose to examine the content. I did not write it for that reason, but I have increasingly considered the possibility that a few or even several might find unexpected value by reading *Gifts Revisited*.

The skeptic in me, perhaps the skeptic in most of us, is compelled to question, to ask what possible value can be discovered by reading the sermon rewrites of some old preacher. How can his ancient reflections grip a nerve, open an eye, awaken reconciliation, help expiate hopelessness and despair? I have asked myself the same question a thousand times. My first inclination is to conclude, *nothing*! After all, although we humankind, especially we clergy type, share similar footwear and ride steeds of similar disproportion while aspiring to conquer the world like some gallant knight, we still ask the same questions while harboring guarded insincerities.

In my old age, I have learned more cleverly to ascribe limited value to the trendy catchphrases and insights profoundly uttered by amateur psychologists, but I must confess, their boisterous counsel to *get over yourself* resonates with me. All of us can, if we are open and sincere, if we clear the clutter from our egos and open ourselves to the raw truth, discover value from someone else's quest for deeper understanding and a healthier promise for the future. We may, in fact, need to get over ourselves before the journey can legitimately begin. You should come to recognize that my excursion to the places of origin, my exposure to authentic moments of faith where circumstance no longer restrained the power and persuasion of God can similarly be the place at which you too can find pause, repair uncalculating remorse, strangely taste again hope, and garner a renewed and promising optimism for life.

My revisit can be, for each of you, a singular illustration to reinvigorate vanishing hope and to discover illusive security. It can confront the lingering need for forgiveness for which some who have wounded others and/or has been wounded by others aspires. To be sure, my journey will, more than likely, not provide exact value or concise, meaningful replication, but it can, and hopefully will, provide a semblance of instruction by which each of you can discover your own reward. I wish you luck. More importantly, I willingly venture to risk saying that you will discover, by examining my points of reference, a place of origin from which clarity might appear, bringing, if nothing else, momentary brilliance, light piercingly strong and vibrant.

You may not fully appreciate nor fully agree with many of my theological assumptions; you may possibly harbor only a transitory and illusive agreement masquerading in causal speculation. Most *ecclesaholics*, all wounded and frequently suffocating from the dross of a wandering spirit, can, if they venture to do so, quench thirst from a variety of Holy Spirit inspired reservoirs. There may be in my revisit a nugget or two from which you can mine an ore of promising certitude, perhaps a single thought that might serve to alter your thinking and provide direction to shape a more rewarding and promising future. Reward can come from the effort to discover your place for a revisit. I really cannot successfully argue that had I read such a book during my earlier days, I might have made better and God-directed choices. Who knows? Maybe *Gift Revisited* will find a place on the inexhaustive suggested-reading-list for first year seminary students.

In a hundred different ways, attempts have been made to underscore and to affirm the possibilities held by a revisit. Your list can mercifully exceed mine, may even gather an endless array, an unimagined appearance of spontaneous and surprising reflections. It may be only one faint and vanishing place of origin, a destination surprisingly discovered on the spinning globe of a lingering imagination. Your Bethel experience can be fashioned by many happy and promising moments, by times when God appeared, when faith and the day-to-day emerged like the breaking of a new dawn, with the extending of new possibilities, a cascading of miracles marching in cadence, aligned in flawless symmetry and purpose.

Chapter 5

Deceptions of the Mind

THE MIND CAN BE a conflagration of endless and ceaseless memories. It can and often does wander with disconcerting ambivalence, causing us to remember what we do not need to remember and convincing us to forget what we should not forget. The problem is that we usually tend to mix and match both extremes, resulting in a quandary of reflections. It appears that this phenomenon has, over the passing of time, evolved with greater intensity. What I choose to remember can have a negative influence on the certitude and value of the present moment.

Age has the advantage of experience and the disadvantage of untwisting, without any sustaining accuracy, the complexities and the disconcerting moments of our pasts. So many places and events waffle along in our minds, leaving us with uncertainty or lack of clarity and exactness. Others are consuming, never releasing us from lingering guilt or the crippling influences of remorse. They surface often, are never silent, and are always bothersome. They invite interruption and forever cause distraction, altering and misshaping the securities of the faith to which we so desperately hold.

The message is reasonably simple. We humankind are so easily consumed by the past that we find it nearly impossible to adequately embrace the pleasures and meaning of the place in time at which we currently reside, the foundations on which we are permitted to stand. There will always be a place and a time for memories, but if we are not careful, they can become debilitating and, with a remorseful hum, orchestrate a melody of dissonance, drowning out the harmonies of life to which we should be inextricably connected.

Those truckers who endure the long-haul across open, seemingly endless roads all too often come to the end of a day's journey disturbingly shaken. They suddenly recognize the absence in their mind of exact, definable memory, unable to recall with clarity the sights and sounds along the familiar roads over which they journeyed from location A to destination B.

Why do these places and sights by which the trucker has so often driven now escape memory? Why this distortion of reflection? The trucker's reward for a safe and profitable journey has been swept away by the sudden absence of exact and specific recognition. He or she is consumed more by what cannot be remembered than by what has been successfully achieved.

The mind is a strange and exotic instrument of surveillance. The older I get, the more I recognize what I do not recognize. The driver mentioned above usually finds himself in a quandary. He has negatively impacted the success of his work by failing to recognize that his memory of each detail along his journey has little lasting value regarding the destination at which he has now arrived.

This phenomenon is not exclusive to the long-haul truck driver. We often find ourselves at this bewildering crossroads as well, a place at which we lack clarity and focus. The events of the past must be kept in proper perspective but cannot be allowed to alter and disrupt one's call to ministry. We must learn from them by recalling the way in which they altered direction, inflicted pain, deceived and mocked our reasoning, but they must not be permitted to rip from our soul the awareness that we are called of God. The images along the way were intrinsically present in the trucker's journey, but the degree to which they are recalled has no lasting connection regarding the place at which he has now arrived.

The way we reflect on and then manage our mistakes, our misgivings, our past sin can be a testament to the authenticity of our journey. Our recollections are not designed to discolor or to annul the place of faith to which we have now arrived. We frequently need to be reminded of our misgivings and the faulty and fragile roads on which we have journeyed. Past events and circumcises can, if dredged from our exhausted minds, have some value, but ultimately, they must not be allowed to permanently alter or replace the purpose to which we have been called. To replay them repeatedly can be debilitating.

It is not the place and times through which we have traveled but the place at which we have arrived that means the most. Often in this narrative, I suggest that the repair of our past deeds is, at best, transitory. Memories will always be influenced by the ebbs and flows of our fragile existence, but they must never be allowed to debilitate and defeat our lives to the point that we lose the security of the faith to which we are connected.

Repentance and forgiveness are the proper destinies on which we must fix our thoughts. A revisit, a trip back to Bethel, can be of enormous value in helping to unscramble the puzzle. To wallow in the past and to allow that wallowing to demean the value and importance of God's grace is unfortunate; in fact, it is sinful. It may be only when we have learned to forgive ourselves and to accept the forgiveness of God and the forgiveness of others that greater clarity can be experienced regarding the place at which we now find ourselves.

The trucker's sudden amazement upon recognizing that he cannot remember specific times and places reveals a perplexing flash of reality. We all have been shaken by similar experiences. A fog has clouded our memory, and life is suddenly out of focus. Have we not been paying attention, listening with care and in possession of sound reasoning and the articulation of awareness?

How can the trucker not remember the swiftly passing but very present landscape? How can his sight erase from reflection the familiar farmland with animals grazing, so powerful in repose, serene and breathtaking? Truckers, however, are not the only ones disturbed by this strange travel phenomenon. It can happen to anyone; however, for those of us who allow God to intervene, it does not have to be a controlling constant. The sweetness of our lives, when seen through the lens of redemption and forgiveness, can erupt in brilliance.

In our Christian service, we remember what we need to remember, and we forget and forgive what we must. Our ministry depends on it. Regardless of circumstance and the twists and turns of our work, the gratitude we have when we recognize that we have arrived at a meaningful destination can have infinite value for our future journey. For you, it may or may not be a time for a revisit. It is however, a destination to be sought, a place of replenishment and hope.

For certain, we must continue to acknowledge any pain we have inflicted on others, must not deny the necessity of forgiveness, but to linger harnessed to regretful and disquieting circumstances, to not celebrate the joy of the few and rare moments with which we are being graced may suggest that we have learned little from our mistakes and that we choose rather to mourn the process of reconciliation more than to celebrate the direction to which our lives have now been pointed.

Maudlin panic, even fear, can subdue and dismantle the strongest of wills, ripping from our grasp the promise for a better tomorrow. We all have been there. We overthink. Our imaginations can and often do allow entrance into our private worlds where nothing substantive or constructive exists, where we find only fear and a sense of failure woven into a spectacle of ambivalence.

Our inventory of disquieting failure grips with painful harshness our fleeting dreams and can, with painful cruelty, cross through our few feats of accomplishment, leaving nothing to buoy our spirits and causing the absence of any lingering possibility to resurrect hope. The anticipation of life as once envisioned can slither away like a serpent, forlorn and lost.

The plans which we have gripped with intense design no longer seem worth the effort—are no longer worth our day-to-day hunger for survival. Our thoughts of how it should have been, could have been, have, with strangling intensity, escaped the commonplace and now stand only in the shadows, surviving in momentary wisps of aspiration, yet remaining dormant, lifeless, and mysterious. Infinitesimal surges of insight have succumbed to illusion; they have melted in rapid and hasty ferocity.

The day Jack called, my weed-pulling and muddled amateur trimming exercise yielded such reflections as noted above, tracing a panorama of life, outlining in meticulous, often sordid detail those veiled and vanishing accomplishments—a reminder that many times, my walk of faith was insincere and misshapen. In contemplative moments, life can suddenly appear cluttered with a corrosive collection of unresolved and penetrating superlatives, producing the dissatisfactions of failure and retreat.

This inventory of one's life can attract unwanted and recalcitrant thinking and can lead to bleak, cloudy and irreconcilable feelings of defeat. We must not allow this line of reasoning to overly diminish our purpose. Perhaps with a timely phone call from a friend, you can be directed to the place for a revisit, not a dramatically altered juncture for service, but at least a much clearer and sustaining lens through which to view each day and by which to draft a healthier design for the purpose to which God has called you.

When one is deep in thought, if the searching is diligent, the prayer genuinely earnest, the reflections deep and personal, the destination for a revisit can appear. Please, I encourage each to search for what, at any moment in time, may be waiting for you. If you are honest with yourself, not only will a revisit be inviting but necessary. It can be discovered only if you are willing to desire it, have honestly and thoroughly explored the deeper cavities of your consciousness, have not forgotten, as is so often true of each traveler, the sights and sounds of the fury to which you have succumbed. The inventory of the soul is fearfully painful. It can, however, when thoroughly and honestly done, when each marginal space is cleansed and forgiven, bring a peace that is sustaining, a blessing that has lasting value.

Overly focusing on past mistakes can be equally as damaging as spending inordinate time glossing them over, as if we are innocent of all misgivings. In my thinking, the question to ask becomes clear: Are my conclusions and reflections of my own engineering or are they of some satanic trickery or are they, at this moment in time, a message from God? To ultimately ferret through foreboding valleys of confusion and lingering guilt, a return to Bethel might provide, at least, a few of the long-awaited answers for which you have so desperately been searching.

Chapter 6

Inevitability of Distress

Everyone in ministry understands the inevitability of disconcerting, disabling bewilderment, the loss of a dispelling sense of value. The temptation to acquiesce to prideful misdirection is abundant. Who can deny that evil, like a roaring lion, has free range on our palatial and self-centered territory. Temptations in various forms can slice into seasons of unproductivity, but can also abruptly wedge into profitable accomplishment. Sadly, they appear often out of nowhere, and some glaringly overtake and supplant when resolves are weakened and objectives unguarded. Some can end a ministry, seemingly sealing one's destiny and driving corroded and rusty nails into the coffins of uninspired and unguarded lives. We cannot ignore the reality. They can disrupt, alter, or change focus in ministry—even cancel it out as if foreshadowed by some ghoulish nightmare. Times when one feels disenfranchised or wounded can overtake the pleasures and joys resident in their work.

This book is a do-over. While I once considered its content autobiographical, it has now evolved into a less confessional treatise and has now transitioned into a devotional and teaching discourse. I want its readers to walk with me, to see with greater clarity the immutable rewards my revisit yielded. I hope they can understand more deeply how I peer, with a new set of eyes, into critical passages, scriptures that have been crucially important to my faith-walk and to my connectedness with a living and influential God. Fifty years ago, these scriptures stood intrinsic in the formation of my theology, helping to balance the uncertainties and the complexities of existence. My exposure to some old sermons released the mournful clutches of blind wandering.

Inevitability of Distress

Some might logically question how the expansion of those stale and outdated manuscripts can translate into a helpful discourse for those whose past mistakes, hours of pain and defeat and moments of despair are dramatically different from those of the writer. Some may feel the need to disarm my meandering discourse and view it only as an effort to sensationalize, to dramatize my self-conferred preaching talent, to shift the focus from God to myself. Although I can understand the reasoning, please do not travel this staggering path of indictment. For certain, I have attempted to polish style, to display some level of scholarship, and to use emotionally elegant expression; this, however, should not be the point of reference for judgement. My spiritual pilgrimage is not tainted by journalistic rhetoric or diffused by shades of insincerity. In these writings, my heart is again open and transparent. My faith is on display—failure and frustration, calm and peace, a renewed understanding that abides in the heart and finds shape and substance in the living Word of God.

Your revisit, should you honestly be open to one of your own, will be personalized and unique. It may hold some modest resemblance to mine but, in the end, it can only be fully enacted by a willingness to yield to God's truth. You must seek a Godly strength as you once knew it and be open to experiencing it once more. Allow me to affirm your suspicions, your possibly accurate and acceptable hesitancies. You are right! We each stand emotionally on islands unique to us and are succinctly defined by circumstances personal and fearfully fortuitus. You rightfully can close the door to someone who insists that he knows how you feel and shares with you in your pain and anxiety. Is my theology, my logic flawless? No! Whose can be? Each word addresses the turns and twists of a journey of faith, chronicling an unwavering resilience for faith in a God who, in our hour of need is never far away.

Most find it necessary to return to Bethel—the often-obscure origin of forgotten memories. It may be difficult to understand the connection, but the meaning of life and of one's ministry may nevertheless be there. A revisit may be the only remaining hope if your ministry has leaped so far off the rails that your work is smothered in frustration and has become the victim of uniformity. For each, more than a handful of great passages can brighten the horizons, invite hope to replenish our purpose, redefine our station in God's providence and purpose. Many Holy Scriptures, God-wink moments in time, can take us back to Bethel, to places of divine encounter. Your revisit can easily open the door, release bewilderment, and unlock the mysterious, confusing, and rebellious stages of life. My revisit may help inspire your own journey back to those moments where despair can be replaced by hope, where your life and your faith can have an enduring value.

Most of us have had moments of defeat or failure. We have mourned them. Too often we have ignored, even denied, that they have marred our thin layers of emotional resilience and pride. A revisit to Bethel is a journey each person in ministry is destined to take. It may be your time to walk along with me. Your excursion, your exposure to Biblical mandate may help subdue, hopefully restrain, the damaging reflection of times that have intersected precariously with your calling, disrupting or even canceling out your work in the church.

Chapter 7

The Need for a Revisit

LET'S BE HONEST. THOUGHTS, sharp, penetrating, and often deceptive, can suddenly descend on us, erupting with a painful malignancy. Even if it is by way of our distorted thinking rarely does anyone escape evil's disruptive invasions. We not only welcome, by our own design, intrusions into our lives, but we can also frequently be victimized by the poor judgement of others or by the uninvited speculations of a flawed and misshapen world. More often than our critics might accept, we are not completely to blame for all of our mistakes and misgivings, but still we are left to shoulder the memory, grapple with any lingering guilt, and endure the untimely pain and suffering, regardless of the cause or circumstance ascribed to their origin.

We know and must accept that past mistakes can never be stricken through by rationality. We must recognize that the duplicities of life cannot be consigned to a twisted argument. I discovered by way of my revisit an answer, not complete, not so powerfully rewarding that the future no longer promised guiltlessness or vanishing regret, yet an answer. I discovered a vivid reflection that captured the pure and simple moments of authentic faith, sustained and held by the unconditional Word of God. This image released a new hope, replenished rapidly evaporating joy, and revealed a new and promising direction for the future.

When I read through the old manuscripts, remembering that they had been drafted in sincerity and innocence, a sudden awareness of God's grace appeared. I was overwhelmed. It at first moved over me slowly, became more intense, and suddenly broke with a powerful assurance. More than anything, I was granted an image, a reminder of the joy, the hope, the promise I had discovered in the exposition of Scripture. I was permitted to fully taste the love of my Heavenly Father, the assurances of my faith, and the security by which it endures. The still small voice came unexpected and sudden. My call to ministry was confirmed, and I was allowed, if only for a brief span of time, to recall the joy and sense of value that preaching had provided.

The six sermons I selected held for me an unrelenting vitality, a renewed hope—one that had been washed thin by insincerity and frivolousness. It was clear enough that I had never abandoned my faith even if that faith had conveniently been relegated, in the name of the church, to a variety of less than productive pursuits. Although my writing initially was genuine, sincere, and drafted in honesty, it was not the content of the sermons that moved me most—it was the awareness that the Holy Spirit of God was capturing me once again and for a brief time was extending to me an opportunity to taste the sweetness of his grace—to divide his Holy Word. It was overwhelming.

I recognized, perhaps for the first time, that my journey on the sideroads of my faith was not altogether wasted but that it had mournfully been lacking in the value that should be resident in service and devotion to the Christ of Calvary. I was now positioned for a do-over, an opportunity to expand on and to bring greater clarity to the Biblical mandates on which I once stood. God was granting me the opportunity to rewrite the manuscripts that were then and would be now held inviolate. The essays in this book explore the fundamentals on which my faith was founded and the truths by which each believer should live. The Truth, as I understood it then remains; the new works reflect a more mature but unaltered understanding of the way in which we *ecclesalcholics* can live out our devotion to God.

It can be critically important to return to places of origin, to those moments in time when the intellect and the heart merged in symmetry, when faith and truth formed an uncompromising awareness of being in the will of God, of knowing with all certainty that the path on which we were called to journey held ultimate promise and security. For me, that affirmation was again discovered in my exposure to those ancient manuscripts. It was not just the pages of writing from which my miracle emerged. It was more. It was the knowledge that in all my imperfections and misguided thinking, God still has a purpose for my life. I recognized that he has a plan, one that is to be held with resolve, regardless of fear or my reluctance.

Chapter 8

Revisit, To What Purpose?

CLERGY MUST ACCEPT THE reality that too many can fall into the miry and hazardous swamps that strangle and maim even the most honorable and courageous, the gifted and those who aspire to greatness. When a man has forgotten that he is the apple of God's eye, that he is purchased at great price, his life loses infinite value.[1] Many of the dark events present, with messy, misshapen words, oblique and piercing thoughts that can muscle a place into one's day-to-day with an uncanny irritation. They can, with bleak and disparaging tendency, settle close as they quickly decry the spirit, altering and then slowly and surely misshaping every good purpose. Finally, they dissolve all good intention.

    Let's be honest. We all have experienced defeat, succumbed to temptation, and stood idly by, allowing someone else to shoulder the responsibility. We have remained silent when man's unfortunate circumstances intrude into the crevasses of a dilapidated and thirsty soul. It is little wonder that Scripture admonishes us, "Make sure your sins will find you out" (Num 32:23).

    Out of frustration and disenchantment, memory of misdeeds can quickly appear uninvited and contorted. Some stains portend major mishaps, painfully damaging, even shifting and redirecting careers.

    We clergy must acknowledge the inevitability of contorted and mournful moments. In those times we often feel enslaved to no one's vindictive and calculating schemes but our own. We often passionately wish to blame someone else for our lack of judgement. It is necessary to admit that no satanic voice or evil misrepresentation is responsible for extracting value

---

1. Thielicke, *Life Can Begin Again*, 171.

from our search for meaning or in our acquiescence to the futility of life. We are more than capable of inflicting uncalculated harm, even destructive pain, not just on ourselves but also on others.

Many times over the years, I have found myself standing again at the crossroads of despair, suddenly but surely bearing the burden of lingering guilt, debilitated by a confused and misshapen regret. Usually, I have endured the pain by rationalizing my missteps as error brought about by some untoward circumstance, innocently enacted by a casual insensitivity or by the inability to integrate the decisions of today with the impact those decisions will unavoidably have on tomorrow. For most of us, that reasoning rings clear enough, so we limp on, never completely successful at ushering the memories back into hiding. Good intentions, a remorseful heart, the perceived anticipation of future obedience is never enough to completely extract the pain from selfishness and pride.

I have learned, at last, that any hope for abiding peace, for enduring moments of contentment, for awareness of sustaining forgiveness exists not in some remote and invisible residence of intellectual and stimulating reflection but can surprisingly and suddenly be discovered in a journey, a revisit. This voyage is not to an exotic land of mystic recompense but can mysteriously happen when we find release from our stubborn and rebellious nature, as we listen again to the still small voice of God. That longed for but mostly ignored destination might be reached through a journey back to a time and moment when we quietly stood peering into the face of God, enshrouded by a glowing awareness where clarity of thought and the reassurance of knowing and understanding his Holiness were genuine and inviting. The journey can reveal an indisputable awareness of his presence, an occasion that cannot be dampened. It can provide a moment in time where light is enduring.

For me, thumbing through some old manuscripts brought that light back into focus. I was reminded of a familiar time when I recognized the genuineness and sincerity of my faith, a time in which I inexhaustibly listened to his instruction. It was a singular moment, inextricably defining true devotion to God. I stood in his presence, submissive and obedient. Quiet. Words were, from my parched lips, silenced. Each manuscript revealed the grasp of a truth to which I had been inexplicably tied, the standards of divine revelation to which I was bound. Sustaining, once ignored, even forgotten reflections danced across my consciousness, allowing me to relive the joy I had known when, more than fifty years ago, I was entrusted with the gift of preaching. Confession came easily—all that I was, all that I had aspired to be, had been born of God; in truth, it was not the product of my faltering ego, not the fabrication of insincere curiosity or the prideful wanderings of an undisciplined intellect.

A revisit can and will be for each a rare moment when time, space, and energy converge in incalculable harmony. A surprising time of grace may await each who is willing to risk the journey; it can bring comfort and forgiveness to those who have, day-to-day, successfully eliminated from their thinking confession and vulnerability.

God's mysterious and surreal voice can, often when we least expect it, become suddenly audible and almost instantly release us from lingering ineptitude. We can feel the touch of his hand, almost as if any awareness of his presence had, long ago, been hidden away in some remote and obscure crypt of fading aspirations. And then, a new purpose can suddenly appear, without explanation. It does not replace or replenish lost production and diminishing value, but it does lift our spirits and encourage us to move forward with renewed energy and usefulness.

I sincerely pray that I do not leave the impression that every burdensome weight has been self-inflicted by casual or the careless mismanagement of our work or by haphazard ineptitude. Although we all do, most do not need, in any demonstrative way, to mercilessly shoulder guilt for uninvited circumstances, especially those that have come by way of the careless and insensitive actions of others or from the cruelties of a world in need of redemption. Regardless of the cause, distress is inevitable, with the degree of its infusion so often beyond management. A journey back to Bethel will not completely minimize the irritating, painful, and disquieting displeasures of life It cannot completely soften the eerie and neglectful missteps, but it can and will serve to direct us to a more enduring and hopeful future.

I honestly do not know if any path of recovery waits for you on the road to a revisit. I pray that it does. I think that it will. A return to Bethel always holds the possibility of resurrection. It may become necessary that some alternate paths be explored, some more appropriate and personalized journey of confessional vulnerability. This one thing I know with certainty; any semblance, any threat of overwhelming confusion must be entrusted to the loving heavenly Father. I commend to the readers the thoughts of Helmut Thielicke. While still standing in the shadows of a ravaging and destructive war, he wrote in his unforgettable book, *Life Can Begin Again*,

Whenever fear of the immediate future, of hunger and cold, war and death become too much for you, then for a moment stop your crying and pleading. Then in the midst of the storm dare to praise God as the disciples in prison praised Him. For to praise God means to see the world from the point of view of its end, of the great victory of God. And in this praise of God our views of things darkened and constricted by the press of battle will be refreshed and gain direction and perspective.[2]

2. Thielicke, *Life Can Begin Again*, 146.

Chapter 9

The Temptation to Give Up on Meaningful Pursuits

ALTHOUGH OUR MORE PROMISING achievements may inevitably become entangled in a web of zigzags and contorted circumstances, a few will survive the tests of time and become a part of how we best define ourselves. It is challenging, regardless of the self-perceived value our accomplishments might garner, to release the momentary applause and adulation for which we so desperately thirst. Survival and success are destined to adjure the voice of extolling from others. After all, we deserve each praise that comes, each victory to which we can lay claim. We have not only worked hard, but our industry has also skillfully woven a resourceful path, avoiding at all costs overzealousness and the unnecessary demands placed on us by untoward circumstances. Shortcuts, creative adjustment, and compromised integrity seem justified given the cruel and unnecessary demands placed on humankind for flawlessness and perfection. In our thinking, praise is too seldom given, complements insincere, and affirmations dismally absent.

For what seems an eternity, I leaned on the redundant accomplishments of my past and heralded a plethora of dramatic episodes of achievement to unsuspecting colleagues and friends, plunging them to the extreme edges of boredom. Although I now recognize the folly of my reasoning, it was assumed since my day of birth everyone liked me, appreciated my wit, revered my perceptive allegiance to undying loyalty, and admired my imaginative skill and flexibility to solve the ills of life. I was scarcely beyond the age of twenty before the absurdity of this reasoning was thunderously dismantled. It was a painful but long overdue intrusion.

Gift Revisited

Success stories will occasionally sweep across memory with specific, recognizable reenactment. These spasmodic images can portend a momentary happiness as they remind of pleasant, sweet times filled with wonderment and promise. We can, by these thoughts, find ourselves easily elevated to heights of promising joy. This euphoria may be only temporary, only momentarily suggesting that our life has attained, at long last, its proper place. For as long as it lasts, we seek to serenely dwell in this authentic and recognizable place of accomplishment, the place toward which we have passionately marched and with which ultimate contentment will, at last, be ours to enjoy. We all like to be appreciated, to be recognized, to be rewarded for our hard work and the constructive management of our life's calling.

While basking in the grandeur of our dreams, we may be prone to forget that in another time and place, our life may have become dismantled and obliquely distorted by our own clamber and misgivings as we pursue passionate reward. In fact, we may have conceded to an obtrusive discoloration of our will, one wrought by our overly exaggerated ego. Regardless of the hidden and mysterious nature of our reflections, we will be prodded and painfully reminded by a silent voice that somewhere in the past a life-altering choice was made, a decision to alter direction, to suspend engagement, to quit, to invite pause, to clean the slate, to look for new directions tempered by a failing-grade in productivity. We will recognize our dreams painfully encountering a sordid destination because of our faulty choices.

We are exhausted by the burdens placed on us, fatigued by the demands to prove our worth. We panic to uncover the secrets to success, to silence the roars of complacency, and to halt our rapid descent, fearing never to see the light of a meaningful day again. Exasperating tendencies frequently encourage us to give in, to give up on meaningful pursuits, to give up altogether on our life's work. Constant failure, evaporating expectations, diminishing promises, insistent and overbearing argument—they all waddle along in search of confirmation but never seem to locate any sanctuary for reconciliation.

At some critical juncture, the wheels of purpose may have come to a grinding and painful halt. You may have retreated, perhaps out of the fear of rejection or the masked enemy of pride, to an uncharted, precarious, and jagged series of misguided choices. Reasons may be abundant, circumstances too stern and challenging to ward off the fear of rejection or failure. So . . . the inevitable! You have quit. You have not only given in, but you may also have given up, turned to something more attractive and safer,

The Temptation to Give Up on Meaningful Pursuits

more immediately rewarding, more glamorous and exciting, less burdensome with any threat for the intrusive call to self-abandonment.

I am reminded that more than forty-eight years ago, I wrote about it. I pondered not just the act of quitting itself, but turned to scripture for answers, for at least some illustrative insights to lessen the anguish and quieten the fear. I turned my attention to the emotional and private anguish through which the disciples of Jesus went and which we, in our contemporized and disconcerting worlds, face. I pondered the decisions made not only regarding our faith, our place of service, but also our ultimate allegiances to him who stands alone above the fray and disquieting happenings of the world. The following manuscript, in updated form, is the result of my efforts.

***

The sun wedged its way through the office window. The ugly smudges on the partially stained glass settled on the keys of the old Remington. The machine was a bequeath from a distant relative whose name I can no longer remember. The typing began. Words came quickly.

I wrote and preached the sermon, "Before You Give Up," which is found in the next chapter, more than fifty years ago. Although it was long ago recorded in the annals of antiquity, I am ready, in these more complex and often debilitating times, to champion the idea that a larger portion of the content is as important today as it was then, not because of who wrote it, but because of who inspired it. Human reasoning always holds the option to suspend engagement, to quit, to walk away, for whatever reason or excuse we care to invent. It is called *choice*. God honors this gift to us. It is a part of the emotional sinew out of which we have been created. Yes, a few people have strong wills, a firm resolve that might insulate them from the coward's way of thinking. Endurance has been disproportionately handed out. However, far too often, those men and women called to invest their lives in Christian service will deal with self-doubt about their calling. Seems inevitable.

Over the years, the temptation to cash-in one's call to ministry, or for that part, for one to abandon his call to faith, is real. Who has not wanted to wash his hands of it all? When I made the decision more than forty years ago to resign my position with the local church, not once did I believe God had given up on me or that He had canceled His call to me for ministry. I have since then, for the most part, kept busy. It was never a matter of God suspending my call. My exit from the ranks of the ecclesiastical resembled yet another occasion where God would grant, in a loving and forgiving way, a sabbatical to be used, not to scold or condemn, but to provide a time for reflection and healing—time to redefine the more appropriate and sustaining ways by which my service to him was to be actualized.

All of us have been guilty, at one time or another, of letting the curtain fall on things we have felt important. We know the pain of giving up on people, of walking away from relationships, of closing the door on an otherwise productive purpose. Many have recklessly suspended projects that were vital to spiritual health and service to God. The mystery of such action seems unexplained, is usually hurtful, and may be confusing. The fear of failure may have had much to do with this painful retreat.

No one likes to fail at anything concerning which he or she has invested time and over which he or she has some element of control. We must be consciously aware, when the most demanding and critical times of life overcome, that certain passions are too costly and unproductive. There are times when some things should come to an end, times when our resources, both emotional and perhaps even financial, should no longer be invested or possibly wasted. Closing the door can be a good thing, yet it must be preceded by prayer and reflection, never by anger or revenge.

Quitting is not always bad nor is it to be categorically identified as failure. However, one should avoid bouncing back and forth in a seemingly endless series of jobs or meaningful projects, never arresting misguided energies long enough to settle in on a purpose for which time and experience will determine ultimate value. Sheer determination, the will to succeed, goes a long way in defining our appropriate place of service. This is especially true for those in ministry.

Chapter 10

Before You Give Up!

He put another parable before them, saying, the Kingdom of Heaven is like a grain of mustard seed that a man took and sowed in his field. It is the smallest of all seeds but, when it is grown is larger than all the garden plants and becomes a tree, so that the birds of the air come and make nests in its branches (Matt 13:31, 32).

THE PARABLE OF THE mustard seed is the Lord's survival kit. He wants us to have answers to potential disillusionment, to embrace an abiding hope before we succumb to total discouragement, give in to utter despair, and abandon the mission to which we have been called. The story was first shared with the disciples, but, even now, its relevance for humankind is indisputable. The disciples had become weary of the journey, had by then begun to experience diminishing enthusiasm. Nearly every day was launched with promise, yet each sunset was tainted by lingering uncertainty. Visions of hope appeared to be slipping from their grasps, silently melting away.

Jesus told the story of the mustard seed to help with their lingering frustrations, with their eroding dreams, with their vision of how things were meant to be. Harsh reality often seems in conflict with lofty dreams. Even when effort has not been spared, when plans have been deemed not only adequate but impenetrable, something, somebody, somewhere is poised to derail them. We often feel frightfully close to walking away, desiring to search for new causes in which to invest ourselves. The disciples had, led by this man from Nazareth, enthusiastically joined the insurgent movement. His voice had been so compelling, his wisdom and tenderness of spirit beyond anything they could have imagined. Loyalty to Jesus had never really been in question, but distractions continued to elbow into each day's experiences. Disappointment had quietly seeped into daily routine.

Expectations had lingered, but evidence of any promised military conquest was no more than a mystic shadow etched into their lives long ago by prophetic utterance. It had not taken long before an unyielding loyalty began to be dissuaded by some lingering dream for national preeminence. The image of a "kingdom come" continued each day to take on a different, a more curious shape. A question must be considered. Could there have been some frustration on the part of the disciples because any anticipated bounty, reward for their efforts, seemed to be vanishing?

The rewards for battles hard fought, for actions that call for inordinate sacrifice, seldom bring, nor were they designed to bring, financial gain. The rewards for charity are intangible. Good deeds, kindness, and the benevolence of spirit are repaid only through a visitation of immeasurable calm and a comforting humility. Even though tax-deductions may incentivize charitable giving, they have very little importance to the donor, who gives because he or she has discovered a more appropriate and meaningful way to provide immeasurable value to a cause. These givers act from a purpose that does not yield to self-centeredness as they share the financial resources with which God has blessed them.

As shadows began to lengthen over some vaguely anticipated national dominance, the disciples increasingly submitted their misguided aspirations to questioning. They were beginning to ask, at least among themselves, serious questions about the legitimacy of this Kingdom of God idea. Undeniably, they had found themselves as part of a movement, an anticipated revolution, the call to which they had enthusiastically responded. They were instantly loyal, even if the legitimacy and mission of the group was vague and, at conception, not yet completely understood.

The disciples' involvement and the movement with which they had aligned attracted attention almost instantly. Popularity for Jesus and his disciples had quickly grown; not all was favorable, but attention to the more intriguing impulsiveness of the group was gathering recognition. Suspicions, however, were also increasingly evident. Religious authority and skeptics were, with equal enthusiasm, crafting strategies to divert attention away from, if not to eliminate, the popularity this man Jesus was garnering. They wished to curtail the forward momentum his followers seemed to be experiencing. The disciples had each been enlisted by a simple invitation—*come follow*! They clearly understood that Jesus was no snake-oil-salesman, had not made any glowing promises, had not canceled the inevitability of harsh drudgery or the possibility for dark moments of defeat.

There is equally a similar displeasure under which we *ecclesaholics* often find ourselves. The battle scars from inflicted wounds usually heal over, but the damage lingers, often with increasing intensity. We can inch toward the edge of abandonment, never stopping long enough to smell the roses or to see the tender transformation of a life we have influenced or lovingly helped leap from tragedy to hope. We envision our troubles with far greater anguish than the rudiments of our profession deserve—more than the inevitability of failure that our critics will loudly and passionately proclaim.

Although their understanding of Jesus was shallow in places, the passion and spirit of the man spelled victory for them and victory for Israel. How misguided they were on many fronts. They, as do we, failed to fully anticipate the cost of the mission to which they had been attracted. They, as often we do, kept their eyes on some anticipated reward, ignoring the inherent obstacles and challenges along the way. The cost of discipleship is too often forgotten in anticipation of the victory that ultimately does not come, in fulness, until God brings all things to a divine completion. Disingenuous faith has many moments of fear, confusion, even doubt. I am not suggesting the disciples failed to take seriously the mission to which Jesus had called them, but I do argue that service to the King is a very serious commitment and cannot be enacted with casual platitudes or with shoddy haphazardness. We must not ignore or deny the reality of momentary glitches of disgruntling or the encroaching temptation to bail out due to evaporating interest or the residual ailments of miscalculated adventure.

For the disciples, the entire endeavor seemed, at times, to be faltering. Any anticipated rewards for service, any shared bounty, seemed distant and allusive. The envisioning of any reward of ultimate value no longer helped soften or minimize the drudgery of the day-to-day. The presence of an occasional distraction, some misdirection of the plan, was accepted as reasonable. However, any ultimate assurance that the anticipated mission would be successful had begun to slip from their grasp. Keeping one's eye on the prize is, in each worthy undertaking, extremely important, but the emotional and spiritual energy necessary, moment to moment, must yield to an uncompromising focus.

Gift Revisited

Victories ahead are bathed in the sweet fragrance of impassioned labor. Self-activating energy fuels direction and crystalizes the value of the end-product. The disciples had not dismissed as invaluable the hope and evidence of the restoration Jesus envisioned for a broken humanity. The disciples did not simply choose to relegate miracles to "isn't that nice." It was of sustaining importance to them when the blind received sight, the lame walked, the dead were raised. They recognized that something of the divine was present with every word, with every touch from the Master. But did they only see these miracles as some benign evidence that this man Jesus, who talked frequently about the Kingdom of God, was in fact the Messiah for whom they wished and in whom they could place their trust?

Ambivalence, though often of some value, can suffocate our focus and distort anticipated success. Demands for evidence can be risky. Distress can overwhelm when we keep our eyes more on the catch and less on the ball. The disciples were obviously at a place of encroaching disappointment, a moment in time when failure and lingering doubt were beginning to be defined by an eerie cloud of hopelessness. Their resolve for loyalty and obedience had become obscured by dwindling evidence that their "kingdom come" hope was slipping from their grasp. A lesson should be learned from this observation. Do we occasionally want to throw in the towel? Does dwindling hope not give way to ambivalence and ambivalence give in to despair? These responses can be a painful reality when hope is distorted, even defined, by misguided thinking that lacks divine focus and is blighted by self-centered reasoning.

Without question, suspicions were mounting, doubts inching in. This idea of a Kingdom about which the Lord was talking seemed too other worldly, almost at odds with the religious expectations of the nation. The prophets had talked about a Messiah, a king who would bring Israel back, not just to national but also to military prominence. Harsh reality cuts sharply into our understanding that God's way may not be a mirrored image of our preconceptions. It is a fearful thought. The overlay of our ministry, of our faith, can often seem out of alignment with the Lord's design, inviting doubt as to who we are and who we were meant to be.

Private conversations among the disciples had more than likely birthed a few poignant speculations that odds for the establishment of a kingdom were not promising. The Roman Empire ruled the day. Jewish leadership was, at best, fragmented and fearfully misguided. Had the disciples' initial feelings of power and pride begun to fade? The exhilaration of new beginnings is often difficult to sustain. Disappointments emerge quickly and swiftly from the shadows, looking for any opportunity to distract from, even halt, forward progress. It had been rewarding to share in the applause of the crowd as the blind received sight, as the crippled walked. The cheering of the crowd, more likely than not, had generated a sense of accomplishment, the anticipation of an ultimate purpose.

A prideful arrogance may have slipped in unawares. At the height of success, the beastly roars of temptation can thunder in, ready to rob value and syphon away the simple satisfaction of a job well done. Tasks lacking meaning and fulfillment portend only victories through over-argument or disdainful persuasion. The nature of the Kingdom of God was, to be sure, frequently misunderstood by the crowds. The disciples must have, for lack of sustainable evidence, been tempted to allow some level of credence to such cautioned response. Most disciples of industrious and inspired leadership will, one time or the other, reason that they are part of the team and too deserve some of the credit for the good that is accomplished.

Pleasures unearned come cheap and are short-lived. Perhaps mental and emotional fatigue, maybe the failure to chip away at tasks before us, maybe disappointments in ourselves or in others give birth to the question, "Is it perhaps time to quit?" We learn, be it a difficult lesson or not, that we cannot tightly hold onto the joys and pleasures of the moment, nor should we. Robert Burns in his epic poem "Tam O'Shanter" so beautifully captures the momentary risks of over-trusting in pleasure's moment:

> But pleasures are like
> Poppies spread, you seize
> The flower, its blume is shed.
> Or like the snow fall in
> The river, a moment white—
> Then gone forever.

He goes on to etch more deeply into our soul:

> Nae man can tether time.[1]

Pleasures ill-earned fade quickly and do not sustain the intensity of one's commitment. At the height of accomplishment, despair and disappointment lurk close, ready to seize transient joy. We are most in danger when we fail to understand that the satisfactions and even the emotions that we find in our accomplishments are secured only by an incredibly thin

1. Burns, "Tam O'Shanter."

line that marginally separates the product of our labor from misguided pride. This haunting but necessary awareness can protect and preserve us from the perils of disappointment and failures that occur when we feel we are the one, constant, indispensable player in ministry or even in life. Pride is the very thing about which God decrees "goes before a fall" (Prov 16:18).

The popularity for the Galilean had already begun to weaken. Pharisaic suspicion and hierarchical disapproval were inching toward the point of no return. It would take only a few days for the opposition to cross into frenzy, assimilating an arrogant defense of religious infallibility. Miracle workers are always subject to cautious observation. Jesus and his band seemed to attract attention anywhere and everywhere; they seemed, on every appearance, to be inviting insurrection. Rome stood, just off stage in the drama, watching, wielding a harsh blade for inflicting justice, and licking their lips with commanding superiority. They were poised to step in, willing to nurture alignment with any group that would willingly yield compromising submission to their authoritarian voice. Frenzy of the populous, be it from good deeds or from sour apples, can be disconcerting.

Adulation is often temporary and, at best, sustained only by markings of loyalty and an unwavering commitment to the mission with which we have identified. Ultimately, any attraction to a cause, any effort to join in will be short-lived if the allegiance finds connection only by way of an overzealous or misguided voice. Enthusiasm and excitement must never overshadow logic and reason. We return to the myriad restrictions raised by the question, "What is the cost of discipleship?" The seriousness of this question has profound value to the jobs we seek, the relationships in which we place our trust.

Applause comes quickly where miracles are performed. Man is consumed by the tangible, even if misunderstood, evidence of power and popularity. It takes very little to bring on indifference or the searching for other miracle workers. Already, opposition was mounting for these renegades. The religious leaders were sharpening their weapons as conflict and controversy intensified. Even the family of Jesus had begun to hold him under suspicion, obviously concerned about his mental acuity (Mark 3:21).

This poor, tiny, unremarkable band of followers was almost a burlesque of a kingdom, yet Jesus kept speaking of a kingdom. The question from John the Baptizer must have been lurking in their minds. He had inquired of Jesus, "Are you the one, or should we look for another?" (Matt 11:3). That question brought its own doubt, perhaps even some mounting skepticism. After all, this man John, who had been a voice crying in the wilderness, was soon to be silenced. Did the same pathetic destiny also await the Lamb of God?

I have often fallen victim to bewilderment and succumbed to the disciples' way of reasoning, arriving at a state of ambivalence where His ways may not be my way or my way, his. Charles Shelton's question, "What would Jesus do?" popularized in the 1800s in his unforgettable book *In His Steps*, glares at us with a penetrating level of inquiry. For the believer, this probing question must seem too commonplace, unworthy, even necessary to keep our minds forward thinking. However, if we resist allegiance to this mantra of discipleship, the consequences will spell ultimate disaster, but will also impale our spirits and render us ineffective in our witness.

The problem is not our willingness to ask the question—the problem is our hesitance to act out the answers consistently revealed to us. Often, we do not quite get to the question of what Jesus would do. Our reasoning lingers hauntingly outside the gate of obedience. We want what we want, and we want it with immediacy, and we envision it to be saturated in glamor and permanency. The problem is not that we do not have answers. The problem is that we may not know what the real questions are. Listening to the spirit of Christ may be of enormous help and may even allow us to avoid, in the first place, senseless and unnecessary questions. The journey on which we find ourselves can usually be best experienced when we take the one step and ignore the temptation to plunge forward with giant leaps of misguided if not egocentric expectancy.

Lordship, we may reason, is not to go to extremes, or at least we are inclined to admit to this line of thinking. Following alongside this man Jesus is hard enough, much less following obediently where our vision appears obstructed by the clutter of daily loyalties. On occasion, we may reason reluctantly to follow blindly even if the light be dim, but only where some hope is faintly visible just over the horizon. It is a foreboding reasoning when we have allowed Godly logic to give way to our prideful natures.

As the possibilities for accomplishment appear foreign and beyond reach and as promise seems to plunge downward at warp speed, the *Light*, who is our ultimate source of faith, slips quickly from our sight, further and further away. We fail to recognize that the journey of faith is often a blind leap. Most of us are not comfortable with the unknowns of our journey. Doubt, maybe fear—even, God forbid, indifference—slithers nearby, ready to strangle our spirits and trample our resolve. The disciples would soon learn, by way of an empty tomb, that faith is the substance of things hoped for, the evidence of the unseen (Heb 11:1).

It is forever accurate that the meticulous counting of costs must be done. Faith defines that the sounding of retreat has little value to Kingdom work. Usually, giving up is never the better option. When, on our journey of faith, we give up on one front, there awaits then the enemy's attack on the new focus. Human tragedy finds definition when we retreat from divine purpose to personal agenda. To abandon the joy of our faith, the exhilaration of our walk, and the sheer joy of bearing witness to Truth is a painful decision. This is true not only for those in the church; it is equally true for the farmer and the franchise holder, the poet and the publisher, the teacher and the tradesman.

Not all choices to quit are self-inflicted. Some come by way of circumstance and some by way of the deceitful actions of others. We are aware that we should argue the ill-guided council from others, but whether our response stems from intimidation or fear of defeat, we choose to give in, to give up based on the opinion of someone else. A tragedy unimaginable is to believe we have been eliminated from kingdom work by a giant wrecking ball of inadequacies, personal frustrations, and fears from which we rush on, not knowing the good pleasures of the journey and sadly forgetting it is the journey, not just the destination, that brings us confident joy and understanding.

I have never forgotten the words of George Buttrick, a seminary professor who repeatedly reminded his students, "God can draw a straight line with a crooked stick." Had the disciples been listening too carefully to the crowd's jeers of ridicule and disdain? Circumstances and the voices of others can never be the reason to quit on a Godly calling. They provide only ill-founded, ill-advised counsel. Emil Brunner, a Swiss theologian and a proponent of hope, offered this unforgettable observation nearly one hundred years ago: "He who has no hope must hurry. The gate threatens to close, then, all is over: What oxygen is to the lungs, such is Hope to the meaning of life."[2]

One suspects that the disciples were beginning to lose hope. When hope is fettered by unrealized dreams, all is not lost, but our journey gets distracted, if not derailed. The absence of immediate success can be a burden to the soul. The disciples were numbed by the truth that progress is difficult and slow. They had forgotten, if they ever really knew, that impatience

---

2. Brunner, *Eternal Hope*.

breeds discouragement and gives birth to self-incrimination. And so, we ask, "Have I been there; have I done that?" One can be haunted by the answer, but as the disciples were to be reminded, there is hope, divine energy loosed beneath the surface.

***

Jesus told the parable of the mustard seed to illustrate to the disciples the might of the seemingly insignificant. Mustard seeds are so small that the naked eye could barely see them. Critics have protested that the mustard seed is not the least of all seeds on the earth and that growing plants can hardly be dignified as grown trees. The point can be missed. The minuteness of the mustard seed compared with its relatively vast growth made it an excellent figure for the expansion of the kingdom.[3]

In Galilee, the kingdom seemed a speck, too trivial for reckoning. Men did not heed the birth of Jesus: "Bethlehem, amid the bustle of the Roman census, talked not of Him, but of the oppression of the conqueror, the movement of the legionaries, the arrival of caravans from Damascus, and the probable yield of harvest."[4] We are reminded that the man from Nazareth found no room in the inn. Failures may often result from one's inability to integrate one's personal snapshot of the immediate as it helps define and relate to future events and experiences. Had the disciples pulled up stakes at this moment and moved on, their decision would have resulted in a retreat into a world of despair, even defeat. It was time for them to stand back, to look at the larger panorama.

In His passionate, loving way, Jesus was telling them that God's power was at work even if they could not clearly understand it or visualize it, even if they were inadequate, on their own, to fully embrace it. Quietly, Jesus was suggesting that moral and spiritual powers, resident in human life, were active within them, even if they could not see them or feel them. There was no reason for them to give up, for they were intrinsically attached to this new way. They were to understand that there was more than the immediate from which to better understand the future. Jesus reminded them that the Kingdom of God has the spontaneity of a seed. It possesses a divine vitality, the inherent forces of victory. After the planting, man can do little until the harvest, except to pursue other tasks in patience and trust.

3. Buttrick, *Parables of Jesus*, 19.
4. Buttrick, *Parables of Jesus*, 20.

We hunger for the immediate. We want what we want and reject any thoughts warning of ill consequences. It is, however, good that a man should hope and quietly wait for divine direction. Inscrutable energies are loosed beneath the ground. "Soon the tender blade appears, then the ear rich in promise, and finally the grain driven by the wind into the waves of a golden seal."[5] A certain man planted. Is he not perhaps the lone Galilean? Does he not give freely to us his gift of faith? The seed has been sown.

The transformation of the soul, becoming a participant in God's kingdom cause, is it not to be ours through the quality and sincerity of our service? He is the Planter. We cannot earn His grace, only embrace it. Light must fall on the affirmation: a certain man sowed the seed. This kingdom way of thinking is a God-designed happening, not to be restrained or to be forgotten. Clearly, the message appears. It must be indelibly imprinted on our souls: "I am the way, the truth . . ." (John 6:68), and so, we join Peter in his confessional moment; there is no other to whom should we go.

The journey of faith is not undertaken on a rudderless ship. Our work as clergy is piloted by a captain whose energy and grace transcends our meager initiatives, our fragmented and ambiguous objectives. It is only through our faith and utter confidence in him that we can be guided into the harbors of his quiet rest. To accept that we may live daily by this assurance can bring comfort to our spirit and help launch us onto a more rewarding and productive path of service. It is a simple truth—one which may, far too often, be forgotten. When we are tempted to be discouraged, we need to remember that it is not the size of our faith but the immensity of God's power that makes the difference.

Usually, our attention and our passions more naturally cluster around the immediate, that which is experienced through sensory perceptions. When we rely too intensely, too singularly, on that which occupies the moment, discouragement and even disappointment can subdue our wills and leave us hapless and forlorn. We can be numbed by any effort to anticipate what tomorrow holds. The anxiety assumed by over-calculating tomorrow's challenges can render us powerless and can syphon away the value resident in today's adrenalin.

The unfolding of time can be mystery enough. The conflicting realities of a kingdom not realized, a kingdom yet to come, was having a diminishing return on the disciples. Jesus was trying to tell the discouraged band of followers that the secret to stopping the bleeding of their discouragement

---

5. Buttrick, *Parables of Jesus*, 20.

was actively at work beneath the soil—much like the help promised by the mustard seed. Even though it is an unfathomable mystery, in the power of the seed there is to be discovered volumes of hope, the untold mysteries of our faith, and the reflections of a promising tomorrow.

Jesus wanted his disciples to recognize that God's energy was at their disposal, even if they could not recognize it by sight or sound. It was a silent energy in a mysterious realm beyond their senses, a region of endless possibility. It does not take long for any of us to realize that to operate out of our own resources is folly and nothing short of disaster awaits. Enormous joy can result when we acknowledge the immediacy of grace. It fuels hope for tomorrow and gratitude for yesterday. Memories of the moment can nurture and help sustain us; we just cannot relive them over and over.

Repetition gives way to the mundane and can hold captive future accomplishments, making them stale before they are experienced. We must never neglect to acknowledge they are mere snapshots that ultimately remind us today of the utter dependence and trust we enjoyed yesterday as we yield to the energy of God for tomorrow. When over-trusted, they can become discouraging, even debilitating. Seldom can we capture today's accomplishment in tomorrow's light before the sun rises. It is only then that the better opportunity for forward motion is introduced.

The disciples were to gain their hope by simply understanding that God was already arranging for victory; his seed was planted, and the full tree would one day be visible. A lifetime of hope, of victory, of *God with us* was theirs to embrace; they were left only to anticipate fullness in the great moment of the *not now*. Man's service to the King is meager, at best. The disciples were to fully embrace each day, accepting that the growth process that would result in the eternal "thy kingdom come" stood in front of them. Ultimate victory would soon be finalized in Gethsemane as the man Jesus prayed, nevertheless, "not my will but thine be done" (Luke 42:22).

We get rest in branches of divine blessing every day. The pie in the sky sort of thinking is one thing, but the sure and unwavering promises of God another. In seminary I learned little about the particulars of the millennialism doctrines that seep out of the pages of John's Revelation and the book of Daniel. I did, however, accept, in most versions, that the teaching regarding millennialism could not be ignored or swept under the carpet of scholarly exegesis. I was just not sure about the exact truth, a truth that rang with authentic clarity.

Caution must here be observed for fear I might be drifting into a less familiar genre of academic scholarship. It is a difficult topic concerning which relevancy appears oblique and foreign. Please, however, allow for one observation, one I think relevant to the discussion. What I learned most in my study of millennialism was that if I acted with any level of intellectual integrity, the scriptural teaching on the subject should not be ignored, written off as some fabrication of ecstatic thinking that had no value for the church short of acknowledging the tyranny and restraints of the Roman empire. Millennialism, to me, seemed to have far greater import than the obscure and mysterious reference to the oppression from which the church suffered during a specific time in history.

The elements of millennial teaching cannot be written off as irrelevant or reduced to metaphor. Subsequently, we are compelled to accept that historic events as identified in Scripture will, in fact, happen. The specific details are not as defensible as is the assurance of the event. For example, the consummation of history, more easily defined as the second coming of the conquering Christ, will, at some point in time, occur. At this juncture, a secondary teaching emerges. If overlooked, perhaps even ignored, much substance for our faith is diminished, even lost. Intellectual argument may challenge this assumption but does support the following logic. In biblical history, ultimate, final events are the unfolding of divine activity that will, in fact, transpire in the appropriate time and space continuum. However, a deeper faith can be exposed when we come to understand that the event may be repeated generation to generation, albeit in lesser volume and historical significance.

Ultimately, the actual event will someday, in time and space, be actualized with universal finality. Let me illustrate using the figure of the Antichrist. Throughout history, the character of the Antichrist has made his evil presence felt. From the evil Roman emperor Domitian, to Hitler, to myriad other such characters of similar tyranny, an evil presence has appeared. All seem to have held seasons of popularity as well as times of disdain. The influence and popularity of these evil influences seem to experience a balance between their good reigns and their evil, much consistent with the attributes of the ultimate Antichrist to which John the Revelator refers.

Someday, only in God's timing, consistent with the inherent, sinful nature of human brokenness, the Antichrist will, in fact, step onto the stage of history. God has scheduled the event. The reality cannot be ignored. Why is this important? The story of Jesus illustrates, time and time again, how the Kingdom of God had come in the sustaining reign of God visiting humankind. The blind received sight. The lame walked. The broken were mended. Those stripped of dignity and purpose walked with a newness of life.

Jesus wanted his disciples to know that ultimately experiencing the *not yet* was still to happen. His resolute teaching was not only a promise of today, but also an assurance of tomorrow's certainty. John the Revelator called it "a New Heaven and a New Earth." God always has the final word. We can rest on that promise with confidence. We see with amazing frequency the assurance of things hoped for, the evidence of things unseen. It is the knowing *in part* that reminds us of the sustaining accuracy of God's immutable truth.

We do not need to give up on anything that is important to us and to God. We should never forget the adage that God does not need our ability, just our availability. As believers, there are myriad things on which we should give up. If we have applied the litmus test that serves to monitor the continued utility and value of the project, there are probably things, good things, on which we should apply the brakes. It seems perfectly right to redirect Godly energies to more productive soils. New victories can be enjoyed from the residue of cracked wineskins.

The relevancy of the church has never changed. It is the same kingdom Jesus called his disciples to champion. The church must always remember not just that the energy of his seed is still available, but that he who planted that seed is he who has also issued the clarion call to personal service. He made it clear: "On this rock I will build my church" (Matt 16:18).

The methods by which that call is sounded will vary from generation to generation. After fifty years of wandering in and out of the desert, I recognize that the method by which we acknowledge that call is guided by the ears, eyes, and hearts of the hearers, by we "who like sheep who have gone astray" (Isa 53:6). If we abide by that call, it has the power to grow into a full tree. Those "cutting the cord" sorts of things are not an invitation to slothfulness. Service to our Lord is fulltime. When one assignment comes to end, another awaits, the result providing even greater meaning, joy, and usefulness. Anytime we exit one door, another awaits. We always remember the seed has germinated.

Above all, we should never give up on hope. We may never, in this life, enjoy seeing that the full tree has grown to entertain birds of the air. We may, however, find a different peace in the knowledge that those *not yet* moments, when we shall know as we are known, await. When the trumpet of God is sounded, maybe, just maybe, we will recall the parable of the mustard seed. Then we shall know, even as we are known. Even when we cannot see it, when we cannot feel it, even when we cannot completely understand it, God still wants us to be his instruments of grace to draw, despite our crooked, rebellious natures, his straight line of truth across the hearts of man. We remain the instruments, empowered by the seed of his might, to share with others his message of hope.

Most clergy soon discover that service in the church brings a critical balance sheet of disappointments and failures. The glamor of the calling may not completely disappear, but it is very likely to lose some of its glow. I am not suggesting that any sense of reward and fulfillment will disappear, but I am suggesting, maybe even warning, that a reality check occasionally keeps things more clearly visible and balanced. Although I speak more specifically to those in ministry, our struggles mirror the battles waged by many others, not just in the church but in the world.

Jesus was saying to his disciples, please remember that, just out of sight, beneath the soil of your despair, the sum of your confusion, God is at work in you. Hold on. Trust more in that hidden power and less in your own reasoning and strength. Someday, not only will the blades slip through the soil in your journey but will also spring forth with branches abundant on which you and even others can rest. There is a final victory coming, but in the meantime, may we all pray for His gifts of grace and endurance. The victory is his. The good news is that we can embrace it in part and someday, in full.

Where do we go from here? Repent! Every sermon must end with the refrain. Joyful conclusions start with repent. Repentance is simply the act of acknowledging that we are not the masters of our own fate—God is! As we acknowledge our own imperfections, call it sin if we must, that very acknowledgement becomes our confession and our acceptance of a new design for living under a new and profound Lordship of Christ. A small beginning results in a triumphant conclusion still to come. There is energy loosed beneath the soil. No one overhears a seed in the process of germination, but someday, be it in the experience of some present moment or on the Golden shores of Heaven, His way, with all His preeminence, will be ours. For the disciples, the beginning of the transformation of the world was happening before their eyes. Jesus wanted them to experience that immutable truth, and he wants us to know it as well.

The disciples did back away. We sadly feel their pain during that holy of all holy weeks when the "could you not wait and stay awake" moment took place in Gethsemane. "Father forgive them for they know not . . ." (Luke 23:34) gripped their souls as his words reverberated, "Truly, truly, I say to you, unless a grain of wheat falls into the earth and dies, it remains alone; but if it dies, it bears much fruit" (John 12:24). They too, on that fitful day, surely must have shed tears of sorrow as the God of Heaven shed his tears of darkness upon the face of the Earth. Hopes and dreams fade but should never be forgotten. The extending of ourselves, the reaching for our dreams, or our journey with Christ is authentic value. We often forget that truth and cash in our chips and head for home, never to realize we did not really salvage anything but lost much. Great hope and great purpose, even unto salvation, can be found in the energy of God and the staying of the course.

Chapter 11

Substance Revealed

BEFORE YOU ARE EXPOSED further to my thinking on a variety of subjects, including issues like why a good God allows bad things to happen to good people, how to know yourself, how to live authentically, civil obedience, and the nature of God, a semblance of disclaimer on my part is necessary. I suppose the actual sermon rewrites could easily be skimmed over, if only out of curiosity or out of guilt, and no one would possibly even care. They could be read with some disheveled remorse to honor the referral made to this book by a friend or colleague.

Undoubtably, you will not find precise alignment with my thinking, will not instantly gather theological affinity with me, but you can, with some effort, discover elements of similar struggle and conviction by which to bind together our respective inquiries and a shared search for affirmation. Please endure the rhetoric and appreciate the effort I have made to reinvigorate disintegrating truth, and please do not disregard my emotions, the essence of my spiritual journey, before my story has had adequate time to connect, in some way, to yours. My advice is offered; scriptural authority can surface if you honestly search for it, and it may do so with alerting clarity and authentic value. My stories are simple. God led me back to the place of origin, the time in my faith when truth shone a bright and penetrating light. It was a revisit of immeasurable pleasure, a time of reconciliation, a moment of enduring hope. My gift of preaching was not being restored. The revisit was not meant to replace or even replicate the gift with which God had many years before blessed me.

I was permitted to stand in the majesty of God, to peer once again into the promises that inherently exist in life, the immutable wonder of

God by whose assurance we find permanency and meaning. My journey became an adrenaline for my soul, fresh air, oxygen to resuscitate my many years of lifeless wandering. Perhaps for you a similar experience awaits, an experience of immeasurable value. Enjoy yourself in its pursuit, in its formation. It will not be as painful and burdensome as you might fear—it can be present in an active tense, unaltered by pride and ego.

The memories of despair, of prideful disobedience, of casual and indifferent actions came flooding back, exposed in a different light and vividly marking onerous pains of misdirection. Although my disobedience had rendered the gift of preaching inactive, my revisit provided a dispelling release from that burdensome weight, a healthier understanding that invited a new sense of value and provided a renewed awareness of God's forgiveness. It all served, in a profound way, to reassure that I could, in my declining years, in my self-imposed embitterment and distorted reasoning, still be an effective and contributing agent for the Kingdom. My revisit did not dissolve regret beyond an unimagined freedom. It did not immediately render it powerless, but it did replenish vanquishing hope as it issued an invigoration of purpose.

Each sermon rewrite is designed to simply illustrate a process, an exposure to valued Biblical exegesis. I do not assume that your recovery from your moment(s) of despair, assuming that one is beckoning for a hearing, will take place, even marginally, by reading my work. The rewrites are extremely important to me, but I accept that they may not garner for you the necessary value or the same familiar warmth they have provided me. Conversely, I do not assume that every reader will instantly close off some inherent value each essay may hold. I encourage you to consider the merit of my subject matter even though you may have places of marginal disagreement with my theology. My teachings may not be fully congruent with yours, but they may at least stimulate some deeper thought, even build on or elevate your understanding of important Biblical truths.

Sometimes a revisit can strangely resemble a time when the sun is eclipsed with a foreboding and exotic uncertainty. It can be like a thermometer carelessly elbowed off the lab table's edge to descend with warp speed to an unforgiving surface, allowing mercury to escape uncontrolled, unchecked, and disobedient. It is nearly impossible to capture the unleased element. It speeds relentless and defiant A lunge from the scientist is unsuccessful. No skilled appendage can retrieve the mercury; no finger can harness the escape.

You cannot successfully place your crippled and arthritic finger on the appropriate medium for a revisit. Only God will initiate it. It will be brief. It cannot be owned, cannot be captured or enslaved. It will not fully repair all brokenness nor invite complete healing, but it will replenish, redefine, and reshape purpose. It will lay, for all with a willing heart, a new foundation on which to actualize the call God has placed on your life. We must enjoy it while we can, respond to the journey on which it can take us, and most of all, we must listen more willingly for the voice of God.

Chapter 12

How to Live Authentically
No Pretense Necessary

BEFORE STARTING THIS CHAPTER, I have done some deeper soul-searching just to make sure I am on the right path. These last few months, I have continued to seek divine leadership and prayed for God's approval on every word written. I have recalled again and again that it is the *God in me* that must take center stage. This book is not about me. Of course, I often am the illustration, but in the end, I may be the image you see; God should be the voice you hear. I am not attempting to claim some mysterious and overt spirituality. I now recognize that words short of divine participation are, in the end, of little lasting and sustaining value. I am fully aware that it is possible, with a little effort, to piece together a few thoughts, allow them to fill the page, and then consider that I have created a special place for clear and insightful dialogue.

This book is a compendium of ideas and observations that intersect and receive vitality at a place that transcends my skills and intellect. I fully understand that most who write books for inspirational value do so believing that the scent of something holy can be detected—the presence of a fragrance that ascends speedily from the head to the heart. I gladly acquiesce to that line of thinking, and herein acknowledge that I too hold such expectation. I have entrusted every word in this book to divine instruction, and I bargain with the reader to allow me that good pleasure and to read further with some element of hope that vitality for faith and a journey for increasing spiritual maturity is ahead.

Gift Revisited

It has not always been that way for me. My submissiveness to divine instruction has been little more than an act, a drama played out in catchy words and insincere contrition. I have often fabricated genuineness, finding more pleasure in expressions of loud platitude than in the invaluable pleasure found in whispers of confession and humility. For a significant portion of my life, I just hoped for divine participation in everything I did, occasionally in quite solitude mimicking a more structured conversation with God. My praying was often overshadowed with elements of a cavalier man who lunged forward with certainty, bragging that he had successfully bargained with God and had convinced him that any vulnerability on display was genuine and sincere. I too often assumed that my fast forward gear had fortuitously been properly engaged and that the authenticity and excellence of my haphazard approach was fully endorsed by the Creator.

The bull-in-a-china-shop motif somehow relies on a curious assumption that God has, by implication, been invited into the picture show—the theme of which is documented with "it is all about me." This way of thinking has assigned Jesus to only a bit part, ushered in ceremoniously as an extra. All genuine surrender to his will has been relegated to the background mentality. The drama is little more than a distorted effort to smother personal inadequacies, a reenactment of some fantasy where the hero rides his steed off into the sunset whispering to himself, "Wasn't that a glorious display of my talent and insightful wisdom," never pausing to remember that any feats of accomplishment he might claim came only by the grace of God and through the influence of divine instruction.

I have trusted God for every word written here, for every idea conceived, and for any conclusions at which I have arrived. Hopefully I have been listening to God. I have a very strong conviction as to the truth I have written. I am not attempting to challenge you and draw you into a conversation and beg an appeal for validation. The divine authenticity of this book can be defended only by me personally. To acknowledge egocentricity does not necessarily demand change, but it does mean that moments of second thought should at least be exercised and should not be too soon forgotten. Only you will be able to discern exactness and the viability of lessons learned.

I realize that I now have cleverly shifted to each reader the task of judgement concerning the presence, in this discourse, of any divine instruction. This book, if allowed, can be not only condemning of our mediocrity, but can also invite some redemption from our fallen moments of faith. Perfection often exists out of my reach, as in some parallel universe, but I believe this writing is inspired from God and, at least, approaches some authentic value and will invite each of us to hop into the swinging basket on a balance scale and honestly see which way we rise and which way we descend.

I remember seeing, what seems like a hundred years ago, one of the Norman Rockwell paintings that appeared on the front page of a "Saturday Evening Post." The rendering showed an old, probably grumpy, butcher. He was appropriately clad in his white, blood-stained apron, his visor and thick gray mustache prominent. His expressionless face looked upward to attest to the accurate weight of the fresh chicken that had been selected for purchase by a genteel, aging woman who stood across from him. They both peered upward, awaiting a final registering of the weight that would portent either bargain or profit. Rockwell captured the greed of both. The women and the butcher were both attempting to balance the scale to the benefit of themselves. The butcher's finger lightly pushed downward while the women was, out of his observation, gently pushing the scale upward to her favor.

A picture really is worth a thousand words. Of course, the integrity of the artist is suspect: Has he captured the exact emotion of the person depicted? Can the observer see the authenticity of the character portrayed in the art? We see only what the artist wants us to see. Here, I make confession. I want you, the reader, to see the way I view truth with the hopeful desire you will then tighten and adjust the way your personal understanding of truth is experienced.

In Rockwell's work, we usually can make some basic assumptions about the characters on whom our sight lands. Male, female, approximate age, profession—all generally easy distinctions. Next, the accuracy of any assumptions becomes more challenging. In the case of the butcher and the woman, we begin next to draw some personal conclusions. Both appear greedy. Then, our mind might abandon this basic assumption and more deeply explore a broader interpretation of greed. We can rationalize the reasons for greed short of allowing any judgement. Maybe the butcher was desperate, not for unfair pricing, but to arrive at accuracy because the owner was constantly on his case concerning lost profit. Our female may have had a similar motive. She too wanted to ensure the accuracy of pricing. Perhaps she was frightfully near poverty; maybe the frugal care of deserted grandchildren weighted heavily on her.

Gift Revisited

I doubt seriously that Rockwell intended for the observer to chase all the rabbits to which I allude. Fundamentally, he created an image, easily identified and familiar to his public. I suspect he did assume that sensationalized thinking might erupt in many directions, but ultimately the art, when viewed, yields to the assumption of each viewer, sensationalized or not. Many years ago, Marshall McLuhan, a gifted Canadian thinker, popularized the pronouncement, *the medium is the message*.[1]

My understanding of his remark has reminded me over the years that what our eyes (mind) observe gives definition to what we experience. Years ago, my wife, a longtime kindergarten teacher, struggled when it was announced that the school was finally ready to give in to the then current trend for casual Friday, which allowed for the previously forbidden wearing of jeans by teachers. While she had an attractive array of jeans and enjoyed wearing them to school, she was not completely comfortable with the new dress code. Her reasoning was simple. She agreed with McLuhan. In teacher training, she was told that what she wore, how she looked, and how she voiced instruction would affect how she would be perceived as a professional by her students and their parents.

I know most have, by now, let go of any hold on the rhetoric surrounding the good old days and have come to recognize that good taste and the avoidance of extremism in our dress can help quiet any trepidation we feel, and as time moves on, we are not bothered by modifications to the personhoods we portray. Regardless of our willingness to go with the flow, I still agree with McLuhan. More exact—I do think how we look matters and does help the ever-present human tendency to inaccurately append a disproportionate judgement of who we are. My point again is simple. We operate on the premise that we do influence, to a great extent, the perception others have of us. The way we look, the way we talk, the activities to which we devote time and energy and many other points of contact define our identity. External appearances do help formulate identity.

---

1. McLuhan, *Understanding Media*.

Chapter 13

It's Howdy Doody Time

When Moses came down from Mount Sinai, with the two tablets of the testimony in his hand as he came down from the mountain, Moses did not know that the skin on the face shone because he had been talking with God. Aaron and all the people of Israel saw Moses, and behold, the skin of his face shone, and they were afraid to come near him. But Moses called to them, and Aaron and all the leaders of the congregation returned to him, and Moses talked with them. Afterwards all the people of Israel came near, and he commanded them all that the Lord had spoken with him in Mount Sinai. And when Moses had finished speaking with them, he put a veil over his face. Whenever Moses went in before the Lord to speak with him, he would remove the veil, until he came out. And when he came out and told the people of Israel what he was commanded, the people of Israel would see the face of Moses, that the skin of Moses' face was shining. And Moses would put the veil over his face again, until he went in to speak with him (Exod 34:29–34).

DON'T YOU JUST LOVE cartoons? I have noticed over the years that animated movies have been among the most popular and profitable. Distinctive qualities exist with each character. Cartoon characters never change. They remain always the same. In cartoons, bullets move dangerously overhead but never reach their mark; even when contact is made, healing is instantaneous. The bad guys never win in cartoons. Illness never brings death. Marriages, though shaky at times, never dissolve. Kids are mischievous, but they never get institutionalized for drug abuse. A character can down a pint of liquor and be sober before the next scene.

Lying is personified by the hero while never rendering emotional damage to friends or family members. Patience is never seen as a virtue; cheating is never condemned. On and on the list goes. No wonder we love cartoons. They not only make us laugh, but they can also encourage hope, even optimism. Fantasy has a place in everyone's world. How we are perceived by others is really important. We usually avoid looking like a cartoon character, but to emulate their more appealing characteristics is rather attractive. As a kid, I often mimicked the heroic acts of Zorro. I kept falling off my imaginary horse, so eventually, I latched onto the tamer, good-guy deeds of Roy Rogers. Fantasy worlds are much more appealing than the stark, often distressful territories of the commonplace.

We can assume cartoons were scarce in Old Testament days, but the story of Moses wearing his mask (Exod 34:29–34) gives us hope that true identity can come by way of the image we display to our public. For certain, full attention should be given to the spiritual image we project. It is noble, even rewarding, to be seen as faithful and committed. There is nothing wrong with that, and if it takes the appearance of some image that is an alteration to who we are beneath our understanding of self, so be it. There are many positive reasons that attempting to project our selfhood by looks and by action should not be completely ignored. To begin, let us remember that the medium is the message. Time and attention given to tasteful dress and hygienic practice will never go unrewarded even if we adamantly argue, *it is just not who I am*. Even if our words and actions are marginally insincere, our reward is, from most, an honest approval.

There can be a certain value in living occasionally behind a mask. Most attempts to project an image that is not exactly who we are on the inside do have an advantage. If nothing else, this persona gives us hope and reminds us that life is a journey. Although we may not have arrived at the place we want to be, at least we have not hidden away the better self, nor have we engaged in self-deception as a way of life. The image we project can keep us focused, reminding us of who we can be in God's eyes and at the same time enabling us to discard judgmental assumptions of others.

Some of the shame that rides on our backs like a ravenous animal, hungry for nourishment, is our inability to find the best and surest way to project authentic identity. If we are daily dissatisfied with the image we see in the mirror, some alteration to that image is inevitable. Unfortunately, too many of us in the church have forgotten we are called to reflect the nature of Christ in us. We are out of step when it comes to determining how that can best be achieved, so the image we project is distorted and often misleading to our friends and peers. This out-of-focus picture can create cautions and concerns for those closest to us.

Image is everything. Often, as though inflicted by some untoward panic, we yearn for acceptance, and as if controlled by some mysterious magnet, we are sucked into emotional and psychological traps that convince us we must have approval. To accommodate the hunger for acceptance, we attempt to fabricate a more attractive and appealing version of the person we aspire to be. The struggle for projecting the appropriate image is bewildering. Church leaders often grapple with the dilemma. We are inclined to find no personal value from the accusatory judgement of our congregants, so how we look, how we act, is slightly out of alignment with the image God has ordained for us. I am not suggesting that dress style, hair length, or an abundance of tattoos instantly label us as worldly and sinful. I am not so old as to write off as lost any believer who is being himself as long as he understands that the way we look can have altering influence on others. There seems to be present in life an abundance of spiritual schizophrenia, an eerie multiplicity of personalities running rampant.

For certain, Scripture often alludes to this fundamental and self-deceptive way of living. Jesus asked the young demoniac for some tangible expression as to his identity: Who are you? What is it that defines your personhood? The demoniac's reply is systemic, a distinction that can find lodging too close to our own hearts when he responds, "I am legion, for I am many" (Mark 5:9). If nothing else, his response reminds us that we too can have a multiplicity of personalities, a plethora of personhoods that are subjugated to sordid influences, wants, and desires that can alter identity, even to the extent that we may, out of necessity, find ourselves wearing a mask to conceal bewildering hurt and misguided self-direction.

It is a painfully terrifying way to live, pretending to be an *alternate me*. I am not suggesting any of us should travel incognito because we are, on the inside, some sort of a villain who will, with increasing frequency, wear a mask because we are dissatisfied with our self-perceived identity, perhaps even ashamed of our flawed self. We have here a classic refrain: We have, within us, a variety of persons, and not all are attractive. We desperately need Jesus to bring clarity through a divine ferreting out of the recalcitrant and divisive spirits. His grace can ensure freedom from bewilderment and can point us to the road on which to better travel—the road that can yield to the one-way purpose for living. Without question, we need salvation from our inconsistencies. It is not easy.

For believers in Christ as Lord, it may be more challenging to project our spiritual identify than we once envisioned, especially as we come to understand the world is poised, with its vast array of interference and distraction, to intersect with and disrupt our journey of faith. It may not be easy for us to be identified as believers, but it appeared for Moses that his consignment to extraordinary spirituality was instantly and unequivocally mastered by the wearing of a unique face covering (veil). I recognize I may be taking things a little too far but hang in there with me just a little longer and I think you will get the point.

This Exodus account sheds some significant light concerning spiritual identity. The veil Moses donned appears to have had some connection to his audience with Yahweh, the Holy God of Israel. The story allows the reader to view a sequence of epiphanies during which Moses was summoned into the presence of God, with the result that his face glowed. This scene is pivotal. It seems to suggest that Moses was so intimately connected to God that he appeared to mysteriously absorb his rightful portion of God's power and divine energy. When Moses returned to the people, he elected to wear some sort of facial covering. Scripture calls it a veil. We are led to assume that this action of wearing a veil was taken so as not to overwhelm the populace with his spiritual glow. Perhaps Moses was afraid that his amazing level of spirituality might evoke fear or even some level of competitive envy.

In reading the Exodus account, we must assume that Moses wore the veil not just to protect the people from the majesty of God but also as a confirmation of his own empowerment and amazingly high level of spirituality. The veil then became a symbol for immediate and instant recognition. Thus, we see here the foundational assumption from which John Fisher wrote his musical rendering, *Evangelical Veil Production*—a hint of the way so many of us attempt to define our spiritual identity.[1] Fisher, a gifted musician, uses the Moses story as the framework for his unforgettable youth musical, *New Covenant*. The work is still around and worth the reading/hearing. *New Covenant* entertains the idea that Moses discovered the perfect solution as to how to achieve the spiritual maturity for which so many unsuccessfully strive. His solution was simple. We just need to

---

1. Fisher, *New Covenant*.

manufacture and sell to the Christian community a replica of Moses's veil. The lyrics humorously outline the process.

The first step is to structure a company. We will name it simply *Evangelical Veil Productions*. The objective of the company is to launch the immediate production of spiritual masks; the prototype will closely resemble the mask worn by Moses. The marketing is simple. Make an effort to place the masks in every Christian bookstore in America. The question of how to become spiritual is answered: just purchase a mask. The jingle is now written.

> Evangelical veil production.
> Pick one up at quite a reduction.
> One way see through.
> You can see them
> but they can't see you.
> Just got a brand-new Moses model
> Comes with a shine in a plastic bottle.
> Looks like you have just seen the Lord.[2]

This raw but humorous youth musical exposes a serious and genuine dilemma in the evangelical church. Mostly, we have reduced and minimized the problem in two distinctive ways. We have eliminated from our worship and from our actions in the world any singular thing that might suggest we are different from the rest of society, resulting, far too often, in a watered down but socially accepted voice. Second, we have cheapened our witness by overt and showy sensationalism and have attempted to modernize the Christian faith with shoddy theatrical performances. These venues so nearly shadow the entertainment industry that it is difficult to discern any noticeable difference. The question then is not if we still worship and commit ourselves to God; the real question is, *what God*.

We cannot escape the reality that our Christian witness is measured by the way we look, the way we interact with others, and the lifestyles we live. We are on trial every day; someone, somewhere is watching. For certain, we cannot overlook the introspection through which we must go. It is a constant struggle to weigh the image other people see against the person we honestly feel we are. One of the healthiest exercises we experience is an emotional inventory of our selfhood. We can try hard, but we ultimately cannot fool ourselves. Masks say something but do not portend the voice of our own personal adjudication.

2. Fisher, *New Covenant*.

Gift Revisited

***

Earlier I wrote of a few positive reasons as to why wearing a mask might provide limited value. When we become obsessed with wearing pretentious, spiritual masks, we may often do so to shield ourselves from feelings of defeat and failure. To live in this way is a staggering and confusing challenge, but it also places us on a downward trajectory and can lead to emotional and spiritual disaster. We can, and often do, find solace and security in wearing a mask. It easily prevents us from any need to talk of failure and frustration, much less prayerfully map out a recovery plan. When tempted to discuss painful issues, we fear that exposure to our humanity may distort a private world in which we have found some level of solace and approval.

Apparently, Moses suffered some disillusionment regarding the issue of when he wore the veil and for what reason. On first reading of this story, a generalization can be made. When Moses experienced his divine epiphany before the Holy God, the glory of God was so powerful, so illuminating, that Moses seemed to have absorbed his rightful share of majesty, so much so that his face shone. When he returned to the people of Israel, to share with them God's message, he put the veil back on so that his spirituality would not distort the importance of his message. Although there is obviously some truth to this assumption, the Apostle Paul sheds additional light on the story:

> Since we have such a hope, we are very bold, not like Moses, who would put a veil over his face so that the Israelites might not gaze at the outcome of what was being brought to an end. But their minds were hardened for to this day, when they read the old covenant, the same Veil remains unlifted because only through Christ is it taken away. Yes, to this day whenever Moses is read, a veil lies over their hearts. But when one returns to the Lord, the veil is removed. Now the Lord is the Spirit and where the Spirit of the Lord is, there is freedom (2 Cor 3:12–17).

Paul reveals that Moses did not wear the veil to shelter the Israelites from his amazing spirituality. He employs a much more appropriate concept. Moses wore the mask because the glory was fading. Many lessons are embedded in this story. For certain, our spiritually will not be adjudged ultimately by the way we look, not even by the way we speak. Actually, it was the radiance of the old covenant from which Moses hoped to shield the Israelites. Paul more clearly sees in the Moses story that a new covenant would someday be pronounced by the appearance of Jesus. The power of the covenant law from which Moses shielded his people was only a foreshadowing of the new covenant yet to come. To assume that obedience to the law is the authentic measure of one's spirituality fails to recognize grace. Should we make every effort to live by the old covenant standards? Absolutely. Would wearing a self-designed mask to validate our spirituality provide adequate evidence of our true relationship with the Lord of the new covenant? Definitely not!

I would like to offer one sidebar as I close my argument for the authenticity of personal faith. We should honestly and legitimately project an image that reflects our personal relationship with Christ. Great care should be taken to do so. We should remember that the only person we can really fool is ourselves. To strive for authenticity of faith is noble. Next, we must remember that even Moses failed in his effort to obey the law for salvation. It is only by grace man is brought into a right relationship with God and a right relationship with others. So, in the end, our real testimony for salvation comes not from the image we project but by the gift we receive. In the opening verse of 2 Corinthians 3, Paul talks about the authentic way all evidence of our faith is best revealed: "Are we beginning to commend ourselves again? Or do we need, as some do, letters of recommendation to you, or from you? You yourselves are our letters of recommendation on our hearts to be read by all" (2 Cor 3:1, 2). No more need be said.

Our influence on others and the impact we have on them is authentication for the quality and value of our genuine self. We must feel compelled to ask, "Do others see Jesus in me?" My wife and I grapple incessantly with the responsibility we feel to help lead our grandchildren to faith in Christ. At times it is burdensome. We are beginning to understand that it is the Christ they see in us that will ultimately validate the value of Christ in them.

A last thought must be offered. During my days on the front line of church work, I wanted so desperately to be recognized as someone gifted, a person of worth and accomplishment. It was an effort to prove that I had value. At times it was exhausting. I searched for a ton of masks to wear. Most fit poorly; some helped a little. Others faded quickly away. What I failed to fully recognize was that God did not need me to prove anything. He just wanted my willing obedience—He would lovingly nurture and provide the methods of delivery consistent with His grace.

It is painful now to recall those days of anguish. The one singular blessing concerning them that I now partially understand is that God wanted to free me from my search for value. Paul talks about it in 2 Corinthians 3 and 4. Again, scripture tells the real story: "Yes, to this day, whenever Moses is read a veil lies over their hearts. But when one turns to the Lord, the veil is removed. Now the Lord is the Spirit, and where the Spirit of the Lord is, there is freedom" (2 Cor 3:15–17). I now better understand that when we let go of our misguided and selfish wills, grace abounds; freedom is enjoyed.

Many of us have heard the story about the truck driver who, when descending a steep mountain, lost control of his load of heavy equipment. To save himself and hoping to avoid disaster, he veered to the side. Unfortunately, not enough space was available, so the truck plunged over the cliff to destruction. The driver was able to exit the truck but hung precariously on a branch out over the chasm below him. With the truck in flames far below, the limb on which he clung extremely fragile, and the pain from his grip on the branch excruciating, the driver cried out in desperation, "Is there anybody here?" Almost immediately, he heard, "This is God, I am here. Just let go of the branch and I will catch you." After a moment of contemplation, the driver yelled again, "Is there anyone else here?" We humorously get the message. Trust is difficult. Reasons to not trust are unending. Risks seem too high. The pain is too excruciating to consider spiritual mandates emotionally, honestly. Letting go is not always that attractive or seemingly safe.

Must we learn anew to trust as we did in our innocence of faith? A revisit to Bethel can help. Do we not, in fact, need to let go and allow God to nourish and sustain us? Paul clearly taught that it is His image into which we are being conformed. Let us come to an agreement, repent of our misgivings and our feeble efforts to caricaturize our person, and rely fully on God's redeeming grace.

Chapter 14

Knowing and Understanding Yourself

MY ORIGINAL PLAN WAS to include in this narrative a sermon entitled *My Search for Identity*. My assumption that this sermon still existed as part of my stash of manuscripts was in error; my memory was flawed. No sermon with that exact title was to be found. Lest your disappointment overwhelm you and tempt you to discard this narrative, please forgive me and grab a little more tightly to the life preserver of my apology. It is important that I confess my sin and do it immediately. I must assume that at some point, in the distant past, that sermon was tossed mindlessly into one of those recycling canisters.

If you are not quite conditioned to buy that excuse, you would be really taken aback by a true, verifiable explanation as to why some of my old writings no longer exist. I use the word verifiable because samples of this really bizarre excuse do currently take up space in my folder of materials. What gives validation is the clear evidence that a few of my old sermons were partially chewed away by some forlorn field mouse that sought winter refuge and food in the over-the-garage storage space in the house in which we lived fifteen years ago. I am not kidding. In the still lingering shadows of the 2020–2021 coronavirus pandemic, one might even wonder if those chewed edges could have helped spawn that disease, maybe even contagiously passed it on? I suppose I would have been the first victim, and I feel fine, at least for now. Ironically, I made another somewhat morbid discovery. Nearly half of those old notes and manuscripts were penned for use as funeral eulogies. Back then, I delivered a lot of them. Most were reasonably well crafted. I hope that whomever does my own funeral will share too, on my behalf, such profound insights. Okay, my tongue is removed from my

Gift Revisited

cheek and my mind again focused. Hopefully, we can proceed with some certainty that what I am about to offer does have potential value. A simple but very important message waits now to be read.

I never legitimately walked away from my call to ministry. On some occasion, a few detours were taken. To confess one additional struggle, it is important to acknowledge that I have also walked away from opportunities that might have been rewarding, but in the end, my own timidity and insecurity brought pause that allowed enough time to talk myself out of the adventure. Whether these decisions were misguided or not, I cannot tell. This chapter deals in part with some of the potential anguish that accompanies such a journey. The reflections that follow identify many of the issues with which I dealt following my decision to leave the ministry. Perhaps, in light of your personal struggles you might find, as did I, a redeeming light that can generate some helpful direction for the future, and you may discover a fresher, more sustaining hope.

Unfortunately, our routine, sometimes confusing lives seem, at times, to be confronted with more questions than answers. A more exact, more emotionally accurate term than the descriptive *life's challenges* should be replaced with the more appropriate phrase *life's responsibilities*. Sometimes the way we handle challenges is markedly different from the way we react to responsibilities. Challenges have far more exhilarating value than do responsibilities. Challenges invite an array of responses and are generally met with some element of emotional energy. Responsibilities, however, place a more demanding grip on our actions and cannot be assumed with inadequate and haphazard duty. We can dance around daily challenges and garner some degree of satisfaction, with anticipation of reward and the adulation of the crowd. We dip a toe in here, a toe in there.

If we desire genuine satisfaction in daily living, our energy cannot be devoted only to putting out fires and in waging selected wars against the routine and often frivolous roadblocks in life. Most can be addressed with more accurate and organized skill and need not be allowed to, as they so often do, occupy more time and concern than they should. We must, however, plunge in headfirst to meet our responsibilities. There is no replacement for hard work and a determination to exercise appropriate stewardship of time and resources. The things that matter most in life must be managed with diligence and an unwavering devotion. A spiritually heathy person is always looking for ways to live more productively and more passionately. Life is a journey, and we must always be on the lookout for ways by which to live out our faith more effectively. Any lethargy of spirit can be dangerous; evil anxiously awaits any opportunity to wedge disruptive ways into our lives.

The original title for this sermon was *The Treasure Buried Within*. It is that honest probing of the *within* that naturally helps define genuine identity. What may need exposure, more than anything else, is the exact honesty with which our search is conducted. This emotional exercise is usually painful, but a deeper and more revealing understanding of who we are, in the sight of God, can be rewarding beyond imagination. Any confusion over our understanding and how we are perceived by others muddles our search. It must then always begin with an awareness of the role God is to play in our personal quests for ultimate self-awareness.

When I began this writing project, I thought about using some of my favorite sermons around which I would extend, and hopefully amplify, the subject matter. True to my flawed egocentricity, I aspired to discover the select manuscripts that were to me more favorable and were also reflective of some level of scholarship and showed evidence of research and thoroughness in preparation. Not many of those were readily available, so I turned to what really has proven to matter most to me personally.

First, each theme I have developed was a meaningful doctrinal teaching that shadowed my spiritual development. Second, it is at this juncture that this book has become autobiographical. Each of the manuscripts has afforded me the opportunity to journey inside the text. As reader, you will see me. You will get a glimpse of my thinking, but you will also discover both sides of who I was fifty years ago. You will also be allowed to witness the emerging me and the place at which I have arrived today. More than anything else, you will see me as having failed, being flawed, but so much more importantly, having been redeemed.

Initially, as this project began to take shape, the selection process included some general assessment that was reflective of a fifty-year-old memory—one that had gone through a few crises, disappointments, and challenging experiences, all of which had left indelible scars on my soul. That being said, my consideration as to what old manuscripts might yield an appropriate value from which to rewrite an updated theme was, in the early days, random and steeped with emotional complexity, especially when I came to the decision to develop an essay that would adequately capture my life-long struggle for approval. A low self-image can never be adequately concealed in lofty, pretentious language or loud hyperbole.

My hunger for affirmation has always bargained for preeminence and has generally been the proverbial albatross around my neck. The text from which the next chapter evolves provides some insight into the basic need most of us have to be loved, to have value, and to discover that our *all that is within me* substance will, by most, be recognized, even appreciated. As a child, I was never very satisfied with the hand I was dealt. Over the years, much of the same personal anguish has lingered. Early in life, in the privacy of my inner world, I developed some bizarre images that would, when implemented, reshape me into a much more attractive person. Maybe most have gone through similar assumptions that allow for the existence of an alternate universe where good looks, intelligence, popularity, and, most of all, achievement is ours to enjoy.

As a child I took the dreaming so far that I dared to concoct imaginary systems by which such transformation might happen. My mechanics and physiology were flawed, but I often stole away in my fantasy world, where limitations did not exist and dreams were real; reality was conveniently locked away in some impenetrable vault. I still remember envisioning that my gnarled ambition for good looks would be miraculously granted when, in my thinking, I was plunged into some magical quicksand through which I traveled to discover at the end of my journey that I was more attractive than all the young men in my elementary school. My body was handsomely transformed and flawless.

For sure, I was not content with being a scrawny, freckled-faced, red haired kid. The teen years brought advanced yearnings with more realistic aspiration. I had grown weary of riding an imaginary horse, perched proudly on the end railing of the old backroom bed. I came quickly to know that a real horse would serve me better in my Don Quixote quest to live the life of excitement. I became more aware that realism was inching nearer, but my search for value and affirmation was still clouded and still to be found perhaps in the distant future. As I grew into adulthood, most of those exaggerated and wishful dreams became foundational memories, and my maturation process better defined their importance. I could do very little about my physical appearance, but my earlier visions for achievement and success had not been lost in the debris of a world filled with challenges and that, by nature, invited failure for those who were undisciplined and unfocused.

I was to discover a world with enormous possibility. God is in the business of affirming worth. It is an act called *grace*. It was the experience of grace that was on loan to me as I launched a journey to discover the identity God had uniquely chosen for me. It was a self-value that I could not earn—a value that is not accomplished by human effort.

Chapter 15

Treasure Buried Within
A Search for Identity

You are the light of the world. A city set on a hill cannot be hidden. Nor do people light a lamp and put it under a basket, but on a stand, and it gives light to all in the house. In the same way, let your light shine before others, so that they may see your good works and give glory to your Father who is in heaven (Matt 5:14–16).

REMEMBER THIS SONG FROM childhood:

> This little light of mine, I'm gonna let it shine
> This little light of mine, I'm gonna let it shine
> This little light of mine, I'm gonna let it shine
> Let it shine, let it shine, let it shine.

> This little light of mine, I'm gonna let it shine
> This little light of mine, I'm gonna let it shine
> This little light of mine, I'm gonna let it shine
> Let it shine, let it shine, let it shine.

> Jesus is the Light, I'm gonna let Him shine
> Jesus is the Light, I'm gonna let Him shine
> Jesus is the Light, I'm gonna let Him shine
> Let Him shine, let Him shine, let Him shine.[1]

---

1. Ivins, *This Way Out*, 56.

If you did not sing this when you were a child, shame on you. This song has been around for more than a hundred years and has graced the classrooms and backyards of a million eager and hungry minds. The melody has quenched the thirst for the simplicity of truth while, at the same time, pricking the conscience of the wayward. Jesus was probably the first to sing the original version—he undoubtedly wrote it. These are noble and inspiring words. Who could question the unwavering instruction found in the words, *I'm gonna let it shine*? It recognizes and honors the abundance of hope at every man's disposal. This melody ushers us on to the world's stage with a simple challenge to live out the lyrics. It is our personal testimony to Jesus, for He encapsulates the *light* about which we sing.

***

A confession is in order. The truth is most of us feel we have fallen short of letting our little lights shine. Perhaps we have not yet come to terms with what all this *light shining* really means. It is such a simple instruction; in its application, it is rewarding beyond measure. We are shamed into admitting to it, but the authentic question becomes *how* and *at what point in time* is this instruction to be actualized. What are the best practices by which we might shine our little lights, when might we hear the bugle's sound for advancement? It is a conundrum, an instruction that we would prefer to circumvent choosing; rather, we wish to go into hiding, forgetting the value and importance of the instruction. Much to our chagrin, we continue to recognize that the verse will never yield any respite from the world of daily responsibility. It will not allow us any verifiable excuse to avoid making, at least the effort, to achieve the song's instruction.

Many things consume us, distract us for doing life with a God-honoring discipline. It is not that we intentionally avoid allegiance to honorable service, nor is it that we restrain the opportunity for witness, believing that more and improved opportunities will miraculously appear. Sometimes, we just ignore the instructional imperatives of the lyrics. The problem seems to be, more than anything else, one of inertia; we lack the resolve to move forward by bearing truth to the instruction.

History has preserved a story that appropriately illustrates the challenge many of us face. The accuracy of both character and events may border the apocryphal, but the essence of the story is so profoundly revealing that I think it worthy of print. It seems that the famous comedian Steve Allan, of early late-night television fame, had become increasingly frustrated with his team of writers. Allan was exasperated with their consistent abuse of the comedic material he had himself developed. They were increasingly striking out, marking through his material, crossing out a significant part of his work.

The mood was less than pleasant when the comedian called his team together and began to reprimand them for their insensitivity, asking, "Where were you guys when these pages were blank?" He went on to make, arguably, one of the most important observations from which I, for personal illustration, have many times borrowed: "It is infinitely more difficult to go from zero to one, than it is to go from one to two. That is, it is much more difficult to be creative than corrective. Where were you guys when these pages were blank? At least, I put some substance on this page."[2]

Getting on with the job, with the sharing of our witness, is risky. The fear of failure can stymie every good intention. If one cannot find the energy to move forward and cannot overcome fear, maybe the answer starts with more prayer and less analysis. Our family, our friends, our colleagues at work, in fact, our communities of a thousand shapes are positioned to judge our performance. Usually, the personal sharing of our faith experience is the first to vanish. Before we know it, the "Golden Rule" is overlooked, restrained by busy schedules and countless distractions.

The distorted pathos by which we view our neighbor may portend the level of seriousness that exists in our fractured effort to be light to a world that is so frequently enshrouded in darkness. The partially healed, sight-deprived young man responded to the probing question of Jesus concerning the miracle just performed on him, "I [only] see," he announced, "men as trees walking" (Mark 8:24). His story can remind us of a truth, a condition of the human spirit. We may too easily succumb to viewing our world through clouded eyes, not seeing life as desperately in need of redemption, healing of the soul, restoration from the hemorrhaging of our emotional and spiritual ineptitude

***

---

2. No original source for this illustration is found. I assume the story was captured in the abundance of popular illustrations circulating among hungry students who aspired to make a place for themselves and who dreamed of a quick leap forward in "exegetical excellence."

Let us look at a few steps we may be compelled to take. For certain, we first must labor to clear the fog from the lens through which we view ourselves, removing any restricting self-incrimination from which we may silently suffer. The regrets of our failures cannot be fully cleansed, not freely washed away, by denial or pretense; they cannot be clouded over by a shallow contriteness of spirit. They must remain a reflective memory of our error and of our propensities to disobedience. If, however, they are allowed to linger too long and uncomfortably, they will become debilitating and will continue to mercilessly harness the value and usefulness that forgiveness can provide.

The choice must be made. Can we allow our regrets, the undeniable consequences of our actions, to strangle the faith by which we are instructed to live? A revisit can be a reminder of the degree to which we have succumbed, over time, to this unfortunate acquiescence of will. Should we wallow continuously, with no reprieve from guilt, assuming that forgiveness has been only partial? Will we presume that recovery and faithfulness have been incarcerated and no longer have utility, or will we see that forgiveness for our egregious misstep is not an afront or some holy pardon for the frail and disenfranchised? God's forgiveness is not only authentic, but it also has the power to bring a rewarding level of healing to both the offender and to the offended. Until this awareness is fully recognized, any effort to bear a witness, to issue to anyone grace, will be fragmented and insincere.

One of the fundamental reasons we have so frequently failed in sharing our faith is that we have not availed ourselves of adequate resources. Resource is a broadly defined term. It is important we open our eyes fully and understand that the instruction for our *you are the light* objectives can be for each of us personal and unique. Here, I think more in the context of educational training and preparation. At other places, I will address the more emotionally and internalized ways of reasoning, the inner awareness of the heart that can guide us through the maze of our fears, confusions, and timidity. They can help with controlling distress and managing the anger that is often present when we struggle to find excuses for failures and frustrating hard-headedness.

I have had the opportunity to attend many seminars, have even taught a few of them on discipleship and/or sharing the faith. More specifically, I have taught a few classes that were focused on personal evangelism and witnessing. Some will remember clever little tracts like the Campus Crusades booklet, *Four Spiritual Laws*. It outlines, in simple detail, the plan, and it includes scriptural support one can follow to experience personal salvation. *The Four Spiritual Laws* can clearly and succinctly guide a person in his or her journey to genuine faith. Over the years, many such aids have been published, and an abundance of training opportunities provided to hone the believer's skills in personal evangelism.

Many of the available tools for evangelism and for leading others to personal faith are excellent. Some, not so good. I have always been a little suspicious of tract distribution and street corner evangelism. Many forms of public witnessing do display value, but some may unwittingly invite an injustice to the faith and unnecessarily provide fodder for the menus of the cynic who indiscriminately fabricates ways by which to denigrate, even defeat those of us who attempt to raise the banners of the Christian faith.

I promised myself when I began this book project that I would not retell any old preacher jokes—those told repeatedly more to fill space than to make a point. But … here goes one anyway.

A young enthusiastic seminary student grabbed every opportunity to preach. When the church invitations were exhausted, lacking a pulpit, he began preaching on the street corner. One noontime, as crowds, along with his enthusiasm, began to swell, a heckler from the back decided that he had had enough of this young man's foolishness. The heckler was confident that he might quiet and perhaps even shame the young man with some theological trickery. Interrupting, he yelled, "Hey preacher, where did Cain get his wife?" The young man ignored him and continued to preach, becoming more fervent. The heckler, not to be silenced, yelled even louder, "Hey preacher, where did Cain get his wife?" The young man, realizing some resolution was needed, paused, fixed his eyes on the man at the back of the crowd, and responded, "Sir, I don't know, but when I get to heaven, I will ask him." The heckler retorted, "What if he is not there?" to which the preacher responded, "Well then, you ask him."

***

Clarification begs here for an entrance into our story. First, I admire, even go so far as to applaud, those who have the passion to engage in personal evangelism, who diligently search for opportunities to publicly share their faith. Second, no one should assume that he or she is obligated, at the risk of divine reprimand, to personally lead someone to a public declaration of faith. Not everyone is built to stand on the corner and preach or to distribute literature anywhere, everywhere.

Let me share this helpful truth: "Now who is there to harm you if you are zealous for what is good? But even if you should suffer for righteous sake, you will be blessed. Have no fear of them or be troubled, but in your hearts honor Christ the Lord as holy, always being prepared to make a defense to anyone who asks for a reason for the hope that is in you, yet do it with gentleness and respect" (I Pet 3:13–15).

We cannot let our fear of inadequacy keep us silent when opportunities for witness are God-sent. On the other hand, we should not unnecessarily shoulder guilt and regret when the opportunity for personal evangelism is clouded by circumstances beyond our control. Many of us spend far more time fretting about opportunities for witness we missed than we devote to praying for better and more appropriate channels through which to genuinely share our faith. Distractions and natural barriers that impede our efforts to witness should not spell defeat or invite guilt if we have a godly determination to replenish divine energy and to then look for better and more appropriate settings in which our faith can be shared with others.

Light shining is a selective process. Every believer is gifted with the necessary divine energies to bear witness. None are excluded. It is important to remember that light shining is an active process of loving our neighbors as ourselves, providing the cup of cold water, exercising peace and patience and forgiveness to those closest to us. An abiding peace can come when we suddenly recognize that God's grace has unfolded and that we have challenged and inspired our neighbor to find favor in the truth of God's Word. Often that peace and joy will come only after we have first shared, in Jesus's name, a cup of cold water. Our best witness will always find expression in the example of our own experience, in the loving and compassionate spirit of "here go I but for the grace of God." My advice is simple. The most effective witness begins with the retelling of our own faith experience and the recounting of the loving and profound ways in which God has transformed us.

***

Now that we have acknowledged that the call to be light is not as natural or as inviting as once imagined, how do we now ratchet-up a notch our dispassionate efforts to be light? Prayer, more personal scriptural study, and letting this mind be in you that was in Christ Jesus are, of course, foundational, but they cannot, with casual mismanagement, be relegated to the occasional. The way to faith is narrow, and it is unreasonable to assume that we can dance our way into the recital with inadequate rehearsal or fabricated enthusiasm. It is an imperative; we must have the utter confidence that we are intrinsically connected to an authority, the Authority that transcends our inadequate and undisciplined lives. The feelings of inadequacy, the times from which we struggle to find release, can be not only disconcerting but also overwhelming. When all resilience has disappeared and our tanks appear empty, we become fearful that the direction to which we have been pointed is now bleak and unattractive. The bucket in our quest for replenishment sinks lower into the well, only to be greeted by a disquieting *thunk*. The well is often dry, parched, and empty.

Some antidotal help may lie ahead, that is, if we are open to it, and we can exercise the courage to launch exploration. Many will acknowledge that the worthiness of our witness is gravely lacking, that our value systems fall short, and that the *all that is within me* is painfully inadequate. This awareness has a very direct influence on the witness every believer is to share. It is the pathos of the historic *do as I say, not as I do*. We cannot deny that this analysis is, in fact, just short of the commonplace. For any involved in church ministry, it can be disturbing, if not defeating. Let's face it. Most can admit failure; not all, but most.

As a pastor, I frequently heard the criticism, "Preacher, your sermons are too confessional. I (we) need to have truth proclaimed by example, not by struggle." This complaint became routine. It began to injure my spirit, but it also angered me. As is discovered in most criticisms, contemplation and prayer will reveal some element of truth in them. While these admissions are given to establish similarities with the congregants, it is important that the clergy exhibit a life that engenders answers, not just questions. My problem was a simple one. My shortcomings required extra work on my knees before I shared their enslavement through confession in the pulpit.

Confessional preaching has its place. We know that and should acknowledge its influences where applicable. However, preaching should reflect, by example, our confidence, trust, and obedience to Christ. I am not suggesting we all need to be institutionalized and locked away because we are so miserably failing the instructional courses of being light. Neither am I arguing that every believer should instantly become self-absorbed, even arrogant, taking the reins to turn the tide of all evil in the world by a display of ethical and moral superiority.

Perhaps we do occasionally struggle to find any evidence of personal worth. Our insecurities weigh us down. We may even feel that we are inches away from drowning in the waters of injured deeds and misguided hope. I am struggling here not to presume that everyone who reads this chapter is suffering from failure or that all hands are tied because of lack of self-value. To avoid any presumption, I write now about my own struggle. My journey has not always been one of anguish, but early in my ministry I questioned having any genuine value; even now, those thoughts plague me. The fear of being counterfeit slithers, like an evil serpent, narrowly close to my heart.

***

It seems appropriate that we clergy types make the effort to, on occasion, evaluate our calling. We may find it important to remain open to the resources for witness that only God can provide. Knowing and understanding our giftedness is extremely important. The search for that giftedness can be consuming but cannot be avoided, even if it comes with questions and struggle. I proceed with full disclosure of my own journey toward meaning and value. I hope that others, in observation of my quest, may find value for their own lives and for the God-issued call to be light to a darkened world.

Please walk with me, even if only for a short while. My search for identity has been ongoing, but as is true for many life-directional decisions, many significant moments have occurred along the way. Wayne Oates, Professor of Psychology at the University of Louisville and long-time faculty member at Southern Seminary, popularized the theory that a person's life consists of a small handful of teachable moments—times when our wills are open to genuine growth and change.[3]

Oates viewed conversion to be the leading illustration for his thinking. His list of life-altering events that provide teachable moments contains marriage, death of a loved one, even the death of a close friend. He also includes some occurrences of completion, like graduation from college or even seminary. His reasoning allows that these moments find significant value only if we are willing to allow them. They have a mysterious energy

---

3. Wayne Oates is best remembered as having popularized the phase "workaholic." Upon his death, news media recognized Oates as the source of this very contagious and frequently referred to mental health issue.

for producing genuine change and the inclinations for some shift in thinking, so they must not be written off as trivial or insignificant. Oates argues that significant moments for real change are few and can usually come only through a powerful interaction between our will and God's purpose for us. Psychologists, including Oates, suggest that any change in our fundamental nature is arduous, if not impossible, to achieve.

I am not arguing that we defend our ill-conceived behavior as the self-preserving inevitability, *I can't help who I am.* However, I am suggesting that emotional and meaningful change in our actions and method of doing life is impossible outside of Godly intervention. Actions, even attitudes, can be adjusted or altered through the salvific nature of God. The acceptance of emotional responsibility and the practice of accountability can earn some credit to offset our lack of forebearance, but only God can forgive, and only God can make correction to the DNA in our spirits. When we abandon that reality, dangerous curves are ahead; some of them can lead to despair and ultimate failure or even injury to others. Change is an attitude adjustment process. It matters little that we can emotionally or intellectually affirm the process. What matters most is that we do it, that we know it, that we practice it, and then we claim it.

Making reasonable adjustments and changes not only in our thinking, but also in our actions is, according to psychology, the only lasting therapeutic that invites the possibility of a more acceptable behavior. The one caveat that must not be overlooked, according to Oates and with which I fully agree, is that a person's faith in the living God of creation enables the miraculous where change is not only a possibility, but also a significant moment granted to us out of the overflow of God's grace.

***

One of my significant moments came early in my ministry. In the 1960s and 1970s, many influential voices were heard in the reshaping of the church. One such voice came from Elizabeth O'Conner, at Church of the Savior in Washington D.C. Her book and church organizational design popularized the idea of the inward journey and the outward journey. King David seemed to allude to the same teaching when he wrote, "Bless the Lord, O my soul, and all that is within me, bless his holy name!" (Ps 103:1). Both O'Conner and King David helped me recognize a fundamental problem that existed; I had no clear understanding of the *all that was within me.*

A fresher, more vibrant awareness of self was desperately biding me to go on a divine excursion—that vital engagement with God and with self. It was far more than Shakespeare's instruction in Hamlet to "know thyself, and to thine own self be true."[4] It was a journey to know all that was within me: my gifts, my hopes, my dreams, the call God had made on my life. It was a journey of discovery, a quest to know my worth and value.

Soon afterward, the movie *Five Easy Pieces* made its debut. In it, a poignant soliloquy is delivered by Betty, a tragic and emotionally damaged young women who desperately dreams to discover some indications she, as a person, has value. Her speech is moving: "One day, when I was a little girl, I went to my mother and asked her why I had this dimple, this little hole in my chin? My momma told me that when we are born, God has us move by him on a giant conveyer belt. Each new baby is examined. When he really likes us, he pinches our rosy cheeks and says, you cute little thing. When he doesn't approve, he pokes us in the chin and he says, Go away."[5]

It is her concluding line that can deeply etch into our souls the pathos and insecurities with which we all struggle. Many of us have secretly lived, much of our lives, with the same corresponding and painful submission. Betty's *all that is within us* moment is sadly exposed when she offers, "About six months after momma told me this story, she caught me saying my prayers before bedtime. She quickly noticed, as I prayed, that I had both hands cupped over my chin. Momma responded, 'What are you doing that for? Why are you covering up the hole?' I told her I wondered that if I cover up the hole maybe God would listen to me."[6]

Many of us can identify with Betty and feel compelled to pray with our chins covered. We often assume, partly because of our sin but mostly because of our lack of self-value, that God may not be listening. After all, why would He? There is a vast and cluttered territory within us, distant ranges where travel is darkened by shadow. We need to explore it—always honestly and openly. We must allow God's grace to transform, in the darkrooms of our soul and onto the canvas known best as beauty and grace, the cloudy negatives of our self-images. The process starts in confession but ends in forgiveness. John, the son of Zebedee, surely must have envisioned the magnitude of this journey when he wrote, "If we confess our sins, he is faithful and just to forgive us our sins and to cleanse us from all

---

4. Shakespeare, *Hamlet*, Act 1, scene 3.
5. Eastman, *Five Easy Pieces*.
6. Eastman, *Five Easy Pieces*.

unrighteousness. If we say we have not sinned, we make him a liar, and his word is not in us" (I John 1:9, 10).

The exploration can be frightening, perhaps even painful. It must, however, find its place in every man's journey of faith—in fact, it should be enacted with necessary renewal. To be *light to the world*, we must acknowledge that we are sustained as we allow God to define our worth and value. That value is best understood as we explore the vast territory within. It is not easy to do, not commonplace. The territory is uncharted. We are reminded again and again to "bless the Lord, O my soul and all that is within me, bless His holy name" (Ps 103:1). Admittedly, much that we are, we have not taken the pain to know.

***

The mystery of self-knowledge can be disquieting to those of you in church ministry who search for reward and meaning through venues of spirituality that make you look good and feel good but have only limited value to the congregations you serve. These addictions are little more than a distraction, lacking in substance. For too many, emotional paranoia reigns supreme. Some of you avoid the exploration of self because you fear, maybe even assume, there is little authentic value to be discovered. You have become victims of the ways by which culture defines success: who we know, how much we have acquired, on which side of the street we live, the size of our stock portfolio, and the level of the attention aroused by the things we (or the banks) possess.

Please do not misunderstand me. The concept of having things or the achieving of lofty goals has not changed for me over the last forty years. However, these ambitions can be tainted and discolored by misguided wantonness. I have succumbed, too frequently, to the temptations of society and yielded, with little resistance, to the *I want what I want* way of thinking. It can consume, even destroy, what is important in life, which is not fame but family, not success in the acquiring of possessions but the acquiring of a Godly life illumined by the *light* we are called to shine in service to others. We are called to help brighten someone else's journey through life.

Value and status appear to be hinged to standards that seem at odds with the basic charities by which the church is commissioned. Even churchmen may be guilty of succumbing to appetites the world identifies as necessities for survival. In contrast to faith, hope, and charity, those commodities at the heart of faith, they thirst for economic superiority and can be hamstrung by greed, self-absorption, and bigotry in all shapes and sizes. Sometimes, even in the name of the church, they may link arms with things the world deems more important and more decisive than are the daily activities by which they are called to live.

If you try, and if you are creatively utilitarian, you can develop a more contemporary analysis of the ways people define *righteous* living in America. It will emerge as naturally as the next breath you assume will be yours to inhale. The *Black Lives Matter* movement of 2020 strikingly reminded me that I had grown complacent, perhaps a better word is satisfied, with the progress on racial equality made over the past sixty years. It cannot be denied that many positive and marginally important changes have been not only conceived but also enacted. I am reminded, for certain, that progress for racial equality has been validated, argued with some frequency by political leaders who need the assurance that their dedication to reform receives the benefit of the *warm fussy* such changes might provide. After all, it must be true; the evidence for improvement is undeniable because every major city in which I have spent any time at all has a street named in honor of Martin Luther King Jr. We may have forgotten, however, that many of the neighborhoods through which those streets pass still show signs of inadequate housing and lack much evidence that better educational or employment opportunities have resulted from passionate lobbying for fairness and equality. Most of those streets vividly reveal that legislation for real change has lingered in the innermost parts of our consciences but must now take place in the neighborhoods of a better America.

We have never really needed to *Make America Great Again* as much as we have needed to confront the constitutional injustice from which so many have suffered and by which inalienable rights have been so causally redefined by misguided budgetary allocations and an inordinate focus on economic growth for the elite. I understand, please know that I understand, that in the last few paragraphs I have allowed for a side-bar in the discussion of how important it is to anticipate and to enact the vast exploring of ourselves, the objective of which must always be to allow God to define our value and his call on our lives. The last few paragraphs have been, for me, more than a sidebar; they have been a necessary detour concerning which I make no apology.

This is not a sermon in which I attempt to chart a journey with some final destination. I attempt to not only raise questions for you, the reader, but also to remind myself that my thirst for what is right and just has not completely gone away, even with my exit from preaching. I have not ever abandoned the question of "How must I be light to the world?" Remember, just a few words back, I offered that the inward journey to which God is calling us begins with repentance, an acknowledgement that God is the shepherd whose voice claims Lordship over each of us. We must confess our utter dependence on Him and understand that the flaws in our thinking are not only absolved, but the direction of our lives is now to be experienced under a new obedience. That mysterious transformation may just call us to more courageous living and may direct our thinking to reexamine our logic on relevant and crucial issues facing the world in which we are called to be light. It is a risky purpose.

Personally, I deal often with an emotional and spiritual laziness. The pursuit of what is right is less attractive than my conformity to what is popular and entertaining. The believer must learn to circumvent the distractions of the *I want* syndrome—the worldly attitude that is an ultimate distraction to genuine self-awareness. All efforts to arrive at a consistent place of self-value seem to be illusive. Our position is simply to never probe, never question, never be overly concerned about perceived limitations and the hundreds of obstacles blocking our steps forward. Spiritual lethargy is, in fact, a tool of the devil. I have never feared finding truth. Although spiritual truth can be self-incriminating and awkward, it can also be liberating.

Too many of us fear that if we embrace a higher intellectual understanding, whether through science, history, or some compelling wisdom from a saintly observer, our faith will be shaken to the extent that we will give in to intellectual distortion that can disavow relevance to historical Biblical faith. We need not fear any *higher knowledge* when it is prayerfully considered and juxtaposed with our fundamental faith experience and our emotional balance. There are deeper, more meaningful ways to arrive at faith awareness, ways that bring a new and broader way of looking at the age-old teaching which we have held for most of our lives.

Recently, I reread Francis Collins' book, *The Language of God*. The brilliant scientist was for several years the Director of the Institutes of Health in Washington D.C. I recommend his book to any inquisitive and open mind. I am not suggesting that every believer should read the book. I am offering that it is possible, if you choose to do so, that your faith and understanding of God can be enlarged and expanded. Essentially, Collins sees the findings of science as not in conflict with the nature and the existence of God. He views science and the data by which he lives to be nothing less than a signature that helps one to better understand God. Without apology, he testifies to his deep and personal relationship with Jesus, the Christ, and does not make any attempt to discredit any truth by which New Testament believers live.

I risk saying this for fear I might be dubbed as some left-winged liberal, but I choose to do so anyway. I found of interest Collins' argument for a scientific analysis of the creation process, but I also discovered his insight to be helpful in my private quest to know God more deeply. It broadened my appreciation for those who hold a more scientific understanding for the beginning of all things. I am, in no way, advocating we abandon creationism as exposed in Scripture, but I am acknowledging that to explore some of the *how* of the process does nothing to lessen or weaken my faith in a creator God. If nothing else, it broadens my appreciation for the mystery of it all. The good news for me is that my view of the God of creation has not been shaken. My faith experienced, in the reading of Collins, a deeper and more profound understanding of God, and I have discovered it strengthened my commitment as I imagined new and more vibrant ways to share the fundamental truths of my faith.

The ultimate challenge with which many of us must deal is our fear that deep down inside, we may not discover much of value. I grew up with that familiar struggle. It can put a noose around our necks and be forever debilitating. As a child I longed to be one of my many heroes, to have a different name, even live somewhere else in an elusive dwelling away from the shadowy Appalachians that seemed to hold me captive, leaving me with little opportunity for fame and fortune. These melancholy moments are quickly dismissed, but they do appear when self-value is strangled by aspirations that find us confessing, "I am not happy with who I am, with how God built me."

These desires existed only in my mind. True, they would have, if real, influenced my circumstances, but they would not have adjusted the worth with which God had blessed me. What I needed to do was not to seek a new name, but to know who God had created me to be. Knowing that would have better shaped my future thinking. The serpent challenged the first man and women in the same way we are challenged. He planted the seed of suspicion in their minds: "But the serpent said to the women, you will not surely die. For when you eat of it your eyes will be opened, and you will be like God, knowing good and evil" (Gen 3:4, 5). The serpent suggested to Adam and Eve that they could be something other than what they were, namely gods; they committed the ultimate sin of self-incrimination.

***

A careful exploration does, however, shed some more probing insight on our scriptural text. When examined carefully, Matthew 5:14 suddenly can unlock new vistas of hope and possibility. It is so simple, yet we can easily skip over and look beyond its amazing teaching. I have overlooked it much of my Christian life. *You are the light* is absolute in value. In the Greek language, it is identified grammatically as a present indicative, second person. The words *you are* encompass be, have been, and belong.

What I notice most about this analysis is that it says, without equivocation, we *are* the light. It is an affirmation by which we should joyously live, an exclamation of sustaining hope. This acknowledgement invites a time for celebration. The message is clearly embossed on the front pages of our journals for self-exploration, etched into the fabric of our inquiry as we excavate the many layers of our personhood. Jesus said it—you are the light. This understanding can and should be transformative; it can help erase bewilderment and eliminate doubt and emotional inquiry from our confusion and distrust of self. This affirmation must be allowed to ring loudly in the church, for it is foundational to all we teach and all we seek to accomplish.

Nothing here suggests that we must earn the status. We cannot. We cannot earn it, cannot buy it, cannot even, in our pleading, wish for it. We just accept it. We live by it with the realization that it is God's gift to us. When we accept it, we are excluded from the residue of doubt and frustration, released from the standards by which the world defines personal value. Under divine authority, we cannot even resist the worth and value a loving God has entrusted to us. For sure, we can misuse it, even deny it, but we cannot erase it. I love what John Claypool said many years ago, "I saw that the true secret of life is not trying to get what is outside inside, but rather getting what is inside, outside."[7] There is a treasure buried inside of us. "The Kingdom of heaven is like treasure hidden in a field, which a man found and covered up. Then, in his joy, he goes and sells all that he has and buys that field" (Matt 13:34).

---

7. Claypool, *Tracts of a Fellow Struggler*.

Because the light is ours to possess, it is ours to freely use. God has gifted us with a hope that is within, a radiance that we might become the beacon that illumines the darkness of those around us—family and friends and all the injured spirts who thirst to know hope, who cry out for acceptance and passionately hunger for nourishment of the spirit. What this verse reminds me is that we may need a fresher understanding of where the process of being light begins. That assumption begs a second question. How brightly, how clearly, how authentically does our light illumine the path for others; with what energy do we seek to bring sanity, even justice, to the blights of our world? Most of the time, when our voices are heard and our actions are noted, the brightness of our lights is also registered.

People are more than casual observers. The world is watching us. Our influence and example are always on trial. We must never abuse or waste the power of the *light*. Much is to be gained by keeping all in perspective. We cannot hide the fact that we are under the scrutiny of others. To pronounce that we are the light is not enough. In the context of this verse any value to the *do as I say, not as I do* assumption becomes dismissive. Scripture clearly instructs, "But be doers of the Word and not hearers only, deceiving yourselves" (James 1:22).

Telling someone the secret is nothing more than exposure—showing someone the truth is the fulcrum by which we can raise to new heights the drudgery and ambivalence of a desperate world. After all, we are the *light*. Words speak volumes, but actions transform. We can influence and bless others, but we can also, often, lead someone to a new awareness of God. Who knows, God may take us to the street corner, may charge us with tract distributing. He may even lead us to pray with our grandchildren concerning faith in Christ. We are light with limitless value. God has such enormous power to transform us and to use us in the most meaningful, powerful ways, allowing us to experience happenings unimaginable. It all takes wings because of his love for us. We can experience his power, and we can know for certain how, if the effort is made and the prayer is offered, to experience his amazing grace.

When we honestly and openly allow his light to shine on us and in us, restoration and renewal become possibility. When we discover again our true identity, endless opportunities to share our faith will come our way. When we dare to risk knowing and accepting our genuineness, our giftedness, the results transcend all expectation, all hope. "Even youth shall faint and be weary, and young men shall fall exhausted; but they who wait for the

Lord shall renew their strength; they shall mount up with winds like eagles; shall run and not faint" (Isa 40:30–31).

In his unforgettable work, *Man of La Mancha*, Dale Wasserman provides a glimpse of the ultimate value a person can gain as he allows his personhood to be defined by God, not by the world or even by himself. It is a cryptic if not veiled message, but we can gain much by its reading. A retired country squire, Alanso Quijano, sets forth on a strange journey. He proposes to sally forth as a dauntless knight to right all the wrongs in the world. Thus, he becomes the fearless knight errant, Don Quixote. He is off to find adventure. Along his harrowing excursion, Don Quixote meets Aldonza, whom he acknowledges as a part-time prostitute. He insists that Aldonza is more than a part-time prostitute, for he sees her as a fair and beautiful princess. He sees her only in this way and insists she is his lady, renaming her Dulcinea and swearing his eternal loyalty to her. Instantly, Aldonza denies the new name Dulcinea and resists any suggestion that she is fair or a lady.

Don Quixote has fixed his sight on victory. All wrong that exists in the world will be righted. He insists that victory is his to experience regardless of all opposition. It is around this amazing adventure that those unforgettable lyrics are written:

> To dream the impossible dream
> To fight the unbeatable foe
> To bear with unbearable sorrow
> And to run where the brave dare not go
> To right the unrightable wrong
> And to love, pure and chaste from afar
> To try when your arms are too weary
> To reach the unreachable star
> This is my quest
> To follow that star
> No matter how hopeless
> No matter how far
> To fight for the right
> Without question or pause
> To be willing to march into hell
> For that heavenly cause
> And I know
> If I'll only be true
> To this glorious quest
> That my heart

Will lie peaceful and calm
When I'm laid to my rest.[8]

As the drama comes to its end, Quixote is back at home and has fallen into a coma. On his death bed, Alonso opens his eyes. He is now sane and assumes his knightly career was just a dream. As death approaches, Aldonza, the part-time prostitute, suddenly forces her way into his room. She has come to visit Quixote because she can no longer bear to be anyone but Dulcinea, the pure and beautiful person Quixote had envisioned her to be. Alonso dies as Aldonza, the part-time prostitute, stands nearby, courageously pronouncing that Alonso Quijano may be dead, but Don Quixote lives on. When Alonso's friend Sancho addresses her as Aldonza, she replies, "My name is Dulcinea." She insists, "If only you would look at me in that way."[9] Don Quixote has shown her that she has far greater worth than ever imagined. He has taught her that our image of self can never be genuinely discovered apart from the work of divine grace, the act of supernatural power and forgiveness from which authentic value can be experienced. For we who believe, it is defined as *Christ in us*.

The journey to know our personhood is an adventure every person should risk taking, for he, who is the transformative one, has affirmed his sovereignty over all of creation but has also demonstrated for all mankind his amazing acceptance—his grace for forgiveness of sin through the redemptive work accomplished at Calvary. In him we have worth unimaginable. We must let God define our personhood and then the overflow of the process be his light to the world.

A final thought to consider. Are we approaching sinfulness if we deny our worth before God? Jesus said we are light. He did not hem-haw around that acknowledgement, nor did he throw in a bunch of qualifiers. Light is made to shine—nothing less, nothing more. Hopefully, we have undergone a self-exploration and have, in Christ, renewed the claim for value. If not, there is no better time than this moment. God so clearly affirms our value. After all, he created us out of *nothing* and pronounced we are *something*. We are the crown of his glory. What greater evidence is there as to our value than the cross pitched high on the bleak and lonely hill called Golgotha. What greater evidence is needed to reveal God's amazing love for his creation. The Way has been presented, the meaning and value of every man

---

8. de Cervantess, *Don Quixote*.
9. de Cervantess, *Don Quixote*.

is confirmed. May we move forward with a renewed sense of resolve to be *light*! Amen!

Chapter 16

The Simple Truth

CALLS FROM OLD FRIENDS like Jack, described in chapter one, can sometimes be the very thing to further close the doors on painful and lingering regrets—disappointments and missteps that have stymied, even defeated, productive and sustaining labor. These infrequent encounters can mysteriously expose fragments of faltered purpose and resurrect deep and crippling wounds. However, the experiences need not be unpleasant or disconcerting. We can learn from them. The opening of old wounds can be therapeutic.

It was not just the instant and welcomed reprieve from pulling weeds, not just the warm familiarity of a voice filed away long ago that redirected my thinking and defined again my call to ministry. God's voice was evident in the call. Jack's words seemed to awaken me. They aroused me from a lingering lethargy and the strangling fear of uselessness, and more than anything else, they reaffirmed the value and purpose to which I had long ago been called. When these moments suddenly appear, we must listen carefully, must eliminate from our thinking all dramatic caution. A voice will come, heralding an event that can confidently remove bewildering disbelief and quieten shattering reflection. A revisit may then await.

My conversation with Jack that early spring day turned the following days into a texting and email frenzy. A few days into our renewed friendship, Jack made a comment that was, in my judgement, the platform from which the book you hold in your hand resulted. My feelings of personal inadequacies and self-worth were close by when my friend suggested that I should consider writing a blog. To this day, I have no clear understanding as to why Jack made his suggestion. After all, our phone conversation had been typical for the nature of such a reigniting of friendship, not trivial, but short of the profound: Where is he/she now, what about that time? I still vividly remember such and such. To be consistent with the egocentricity in my own mind, I thought that Jack surely recognized, finally, that I shared similarity with him, that I stood with him intellectually and spiritually on level ground. My struggle for giftedness and equality with others often begged for affirmation. Surely if Jack admitted that he had smelled the fragrance of genius in my accomplishments, he deemed me worthy of public praise.

The folly of my thinking need not be further mentioned even if my reflection does underscore the struggle with which many of us too often deal. A few times since I began my obtuse ego-chasing and inquiry into the *why* of Jack's suggestion, I have done my own probe into the subtle reasoning behind his comment. Who knows why? More likely than not, his remarks were just part of normal conversation, one during which I struggled for the right words to legitimize my motives, most of which I did not understand. At this moment, I choose to give God the credit, not just for Jack's suggestion, but mostly for the way in which God's mysteries were beginning to become less clouded. It was the simple encouragement I needed. Although I hesitantly confessed to Jack that I really did not know what a blog was nor did I have the foggiest idea as to how one went about its creation, it was his suggestion that ignited a new curiosity and exploration.

In an email to Jack, I asked what I assumed then was a direct question about his blog suggestion. I had the feeling then, and still do now, that my friend's submission to and utter dependence on the Holy Spirit of God had been faithfully observed, even if he did not seek any credit for raising the blog subject, so to give the Lord credit for anything Jack suggested seems appropriate. Someday, if he does not know it now, I think he will fully recognize that his suggestion was, in fact, a God thing. Above all, it certainly repaired some of my lingering feelings of personal inadequacy as it halted the encroachment of thoughts of failure and the loss of any assurance that some form of ministry was for me still ahead. It even helped me deal, in a meaningful way, with my always-present question of how my call to ministry would be actualized at this point in my life. How would I live it out? I really am an *ecclesaholic*.

Chapter 17

Reasoning
Its Influence and Use

EARLY IN MY MINISTRY I prided myself in reading, even attempting to mimic, some of the more-clever writers and speakers, especially those whose primary objective was to unveil the authentic teachings of Scripture to an inquiring, inquisitive mind. I loved the power of the written word. I admired the many who possessed the skill to fashion a story, one that magically drew the reader into the drama to the extent that the reader would begin to relinquish his or her emotions and become a part of the story itself. In my consideration of my old sermons, I questioned if I had approached that artful skill, in small measure, in my early writings.

That dusty manila folder of manuscripts then became an amazing point of connection to Jack's idea. A heightened awareness was present as I turned pages and explored sentences. I experienced an unassuming pleasure with each word, each paragraph I read. I remembered that I had had the good pleasure of joining God in the creation of those sermons. I recalled that those manuscripts had been written with an almost unfathomable emotion.[1]

The re-examination of the old manuscripts invited not only a metamorphosis for creative intellect but a revival of spiritual understanding. I felt I was being permitted a brief travel on the path of ageless inspiration. Earlier I had emailed Jack a few short samples of some of my more recently conceived thoughts—insights pieced together. I borrowed an idea or two

---

1. I officially preached last in 1980. Each manuscript was developed during the ten years preceding that date.

from something I had recently considered worthy of print or provided an excerpt or two from one of the old sermons. My creativity was awakened, and new and more mature thinking began to break, giving me new confidence. I was not sure, at least at that moment, what lay ahead, but I recognized that a rewarding writing assignment would be the next step, ultimately becoming the foundation upon which *Gift Revisited* is based.

The original manuscripts were birthed by way of a holy inspiration. The new writings would assume the same path for creation. God's inspiration was the authentic voice that made the manuscripts have genuine life. It was the essence, the heart of the emotion that I was permitted to revisit. The inherent power of the words did not come from the writer's skill and insight, but from beyond the boundary of human understanding. I had written them all, but the energy that infused them was from God. And now, my ability to bring a profound, almost mystical explanation must end. Any efforts to bring an enlightened defense here or at any other place are no longer of concern to me. To know God's will, to sense and taste his inspiration, is left for each to recognize and to affirm for himself or herself. The choice to understand and to embrace an unwavering confidence in the providence of God is individual.

Our faith does sustain and provide forward momentum, but even our faith has its own boundaries and limitations. God's inspiration can often seem too illusive and mysterious, beyond the reach and intellectual capacities of man, but it is nevertheless very real. Man's desire to fully experience moments of encounter with God can be and will continue to be silenced by our limited capacities to hear divine utterance. Prayer is frequently offered, our will honestly and openly surrendered to His, but the actuality of intellectually and experientially knowing fully the answers to our inquiries is often allusive, beyond the reaches of our finite grasp for understanding.

We may hear no voice. We see no writing on the wall, but we somehow know, beyond intellectual comprehension, that God is listening. Too often we seek his inspiration under some cloud of doubt, even denial. Often, we are compelled to question our spiritual alertness, our ability to clearly and objectively understand the origins of inspiration that intersect with our knowledge and God's instruction. When those original manuscripts were written, I knew beyond question that I was fully trusting for his will, for his inspiration to be the guiding voice in every syllable written. Life, the knowing of God's will and the understanding of His inspiration, is, in the end, a mystery. Forward momentum always precedes full knowledge. Faith is the motion of stepping forward, a cadence of trust, the hope of some revelation yet to be revealed.

Ultimately, faith is reduced to the simplicity of acceptance—the emotional, intellectual reasoning that we are, at any given moment in time, on a journey of actualizing God's will, of knowing that he is, in truth, the voice that sustains and inspires us. We have prayed for divine direction, mapped out a logical path to realization, locked-in on our destination, and can now have the assurance of forward momentum, at least until some difficult circumstance or roadblock occurs.

We may never hear a voice or see any tangible evidence, but the unseen activity of the Holy Spirit of God is experienced not by audible sound or by the moving of mountains but by the still small voice whose authenticity comes in the quiet confidence that each step taken is conformation of a divine presence. Volumes could be written, in fact have been written, about the human effort to know God's will, to discern his voice. In my experience, God's will is best validated in retrospect—the looking back at the journey, ultimately assuring us of the accuracy by which we have or have not responded to divine instruction. I could count on my fingers the number of times I was wholly and completely aware of God's voice. My assurance and certainty of a recognizable voice has been strangely limited. Maybe God intends for it to be that way. I think the writer of Hebrews would agree in his classic effort to define faith: "Now faith is the assurance of things hoped for, the conviction of things not seen" (Heb 11:1).

I have never doubted that God had something to say. Frequently, I was alarmed that his direction for my life seemed to have been unfairly silenced, perhaps erased from any realm of actualization. Knowing His voice is the mystery about which we must sometimes beg for instruction. We are reminded that faith is best defined by recognizing that we must not perpetually plead for answers. Trust is a private moment when no additional concern as to how our prayers will be realized is necessary. It is in the seeking and in the asking that our faith is best legitimized because we realize God's voice will not be silenced and that He assures us, in so many ways, of His willingness to participate in human activity. All honest prayers are answered.

Faith then is trusting that each step taken, when done so with utter dependence on God's providence, is a step consistent with and in surrender to the will of our Heavenly Father. Faith is not knowing God's will as much as it is experiencing God's will by each step we take forward. We must not ultimately seek for answers. Rather, we must place our trust in God as Creator and Savior. I submit that knowing God's will and listening to his divine inspiration are interchangeable realities; both are difficult to fully know at times, but my revisit of those old manuscripts reminded me, in the most profound of ways, that each writing revealed the taste of the divine.

To most of us, personal moments of inspiration may seem more mystical, less vivid and measurable, than we think they should, but they do happen. No claps of thunder came at my call or at the distribution of God's giftedness to me. No burning bush was present in the original drafting of those manuscripts, nor am I now, as I revisit the writings, swept away by strange illusion.

The energy of God has now, as it did then, overcome me in an indescribable way. It is as if divine current reached into the empty receptacle of my wounded heart. The current took hold and continues its journey of truth and understanding. Intellectually, the point is made. You must then determine if you are content with the mystery of it all. Time washes away the emotion, but the images remain. The calls from God come quickly. They come quietly. Some fade. Some will remain beyond the end of our journey on earth. Some are lost. Some we are allowed to revisit. In life the chance of a redo is at best, slim. When we mismanage opportunities, they most often vanish. The repair of a broken opportunity can be costly. Most epoxies are cheaply made and short of perfection. That is not to say that we should not try to fix things; sincere effort finds reward. Winding back the clock, however, is often only an illusion. The inevitability of such an exercise must be accepted.

He who repairs human brokenness must be consulted for any genuine makeover. I have openly sought God's leadership in the exercising of this revisit project. I lean again on him who guides us through the twisted valleys of our frail existence for he is truly the Way and the Truth that leads to authentic understanding. For certain, his grace allows a journey back to Bethel. It brings a much-needed experience that sustains and even strengthens us with a divine resilience. We must not rely on such an excursion for ultimate reinstatement, but it is good to revisit. My sincere prayer is that you are enjoying with me this short jaunt. We can all learn much together.

Chapter 18

A Godlier Reasoning

As the title of this book suggests, I was many months ago provided the chance to reconnect to a time when God was most real to me, a time unencumbered by questions for which there were no answers. It was an innocent time during which the exhilaration and the joy of preaching was unblemished by my pride and egocentricity. Early in my ministry, preaching held for me enormous value. Shortly before graduating from seminary, I was distressed by my preaching professor's response when I informed him that I had accepted the position of Associate Pastor for Youth and Education with a reasonably large church. He seemed disappointed, unnecessarily agitated.

His class was the highlight of my seminary experience and had served to confirm my love for the pulpit. A full-length manuscript was required, and the grade was privately discussed at the professor's residence. I received an A on the sermon manuscript and was even more honored when George Buttrick, the professor, remarked that he had taught preaching for forty years at Harvard and gave very few A grades. I came down only slightly when he further remarked that he gave me the grade not because I deserved it, but because I had risked investing myself in some very challenging theological questions.

If nothing else, that conversation was an assumption, at least for my professor, that the major talent on which I should concentrate was preaching. His unwillingness to celebrate my appointment as an associate pastor should not have been a surprise. I relate this story not because I got the A on my full-length manuscript—there were other papers on which he penciled, "I am very disappointed, especially after the A on your sermon." I tell the story because of where my passion for the pulpit had, early in my life, settled. Until recently, that passion was filed away, reassigned to other activity. When I walked away from my last pastoral assignment, I willingly accepted the harsh reality that the gift of proclamation was no longer mine, no longer existed, was not to be used as an expression of my relationship with God.

The search for answers to life's most troubling questions, regardless of the intensity and sincerity of our pleading and our bargaining for clarity, can leave us empty and defeated. When we come to the place where we demand answers, our frustrations and our arguments can place us on a ruinous and desperate road to greater and more severely maligned inquiry. It is especially then that a revisit is needed. Seldom is adequate light shed on our beleaguered inquisitiveness. Seldom, if ever, will the unquenchable thirst for understanding magically be satisfied. It comes only as we allow God to confront our self-designed steps of hopelessness and halt our rush to certain futility. It may only be at that place of contrition that some light can break. A revisit can shed light, engendering a deeper understanding of ourselves, our place, and our purpose.

It must be recognized that any revisit one enjoys is not designed to clear all the debris, but it can become a compass directing each to his true north, his rightful place in service to the King. It must be cautioned that a revisit will not reveal all the answers. Although each person's journey is to be understood as a pilgrimage fraught with an aura of disenchantment, a revisit can, through Godly intervention, repair damage done by lingering distress that is weighty and worrisome. A revisit can remind us of the nature of grace. It is always a good thing to experience a brief glance into the mystery of it all, a peering into the memories that have helped to define our faith or lack of it. It is a brief jaunt that will not provide all the answers, nor will it fully release us from the bondage of those questions that will be answered only in the *not yet* moments of history or that can satisfy the insatiable thirst for ultimate wisdom.

I pray the Holy Spirit of God will somewhere, perhaps by a word or two from this book, draw you to your time and place of a revisit. It may not be the best of places from which light will break in a profound way on your journey but it might just be the destiny toward which he now instructs. It is important to note that many stages in life are adjudged productive, resulting in some modest and promising reward. Moments of despair, of willful and painful actions, cannot conveniently be erased by wishful thought. They cannot be escaped, conveniently restrained, held captive by shadow or by rambling and illusionary confession. They exist; they cannot, even with emotional surgery, be extracted as if they never happened—the menacing, unwarranted guise of self-inflicted guilt can exist forever in the world of one's consciousness.

Chapter 19

Theodicy
Living Authentically Through Crisis

THE YEAR WAS 1971. It was a normal Sunday afternoon, whatever normal could mean for a newlywed couple constantly making life-style adjustments. Both my wife and I often experienced moments of struggle, requiring from each of us an occasional concession to his or her thinking. As if those challenges were not enough, my last year in college, a full-time job, and mounting financial responsibilities threw in their own unique monkey-wrench to keep our lives in constant flux. However, I loved every moment of our struggles, and I still cherish the memory of those magical days during which we dealt with growing pains as well as emotional and spiritual explorations at a feverish pace.

We devoted an abundance of time to considering critical issues of our future—challenges that we anticipated could bring struggles and might require adjustments. For sure, I had more questions than answers, but for the moment, I was consumed by the thrill of it all. Normal in those days probably meant that the ink had dried on one more now late research paper. On that list of issues was the realization my wife and I were beginning to get the hang of this new adventure called marriage. We met in 1969 during my junior year at Belmont College (now University). My first encounter with Linda was short in duration (a brief beginning-of-the-school-year introduction on the porch of the girl's dorm), but I quickly realized I was hooked and my life was about to be dramatically altered, in a good way, by this very cute and somewhat sassy Kentucky girl. We were married within a year of meeting.

Theodicy

***

I was resting, maybe near sleep, in our landlady's special chair; the one she reluctantly allowed to remain in her attached, one-bedroom rental apartment despite the fear some stain might find lodging on the antique fabric and permanently damage that priceless treasure Uncle Ralph had left her following his untimely departure. My thoughts turned to the world around me. How explosive the last few years had seemed as monumental events had ripped through the soul of a fragmented nation. The Vietnam War still held a painful grip on the country. Neil Armstrong had, within just the last year, been the first person to walk on the moon. America's pride and self-conscientiousness was being felt internationally, and the nation was poised to set lofty standards of which the world was not only taking notice but was also beginning to envy.

On the other side of the spectrum, protestors commanded, more accurately, demanded, a voice in capturing their rightful place in the reshaping of a wounded nation. Their voices of protest reverberated across the country. Most youth seemed uncertain about the future long before global warming and economic tensions had planted a more resolute boot on the ground. The Peace Corp seemed more attractive than more time in the sacred halls of academia, but the call to ministry seemed to be luring me to Christian service and on to seminary.

I understood very little about what was going on in the world as well as what was happening in the church, but all efforts to reach for some deeper understanding, some insight, was an exhilarating and rewarding pursuit. I felt poised for an adventure and anxious to not just put a toe in but to plunge into the rewarding waters of the ecclesiastical world. I was equally willing to go to the mat to wrestle with any assumed challenges church ministry might unleash. I suspected there would be a few disconcerting roadblocks along the way, but I never imagined, even once, that I was not up to the necessary tasks of vigilance. I passionately assured myself that I was more than prepared to navigate the world of church ministry.

***

More than a few times in the early 1970s, I envisioned myself at a peace rally or a civil rights march. For some of us, back then, emotional and spiritual energy was abundant. More fortunately, God was first to claim

Gift Revisited

the value of that energy, and my focus and call to ministry were not at risk. Soon, with college graduation just a few breaths and research papers away, most of my social and political passions were arrested and seminary work began to cloud over any misappropriation of social conscientiousness.

Many critical issues occupied my mind during my years at Belmont. There were issues with which I struggled, but also significant questions whose illusive answers did little to alter my thinking or to expand my perception for the way of life into which God was calling me. Some understanding of the shape my work was to take had burned a deep and permanent place in my soul. Any attempt to explain how a benevolent, loving God could allow evil a foothold in the world was a question with which I was destined to grapple throughout my ministry.

My waxing eloquently about the mysteries of the universe was, in truth, exhausting and usually, within minutes of conception, eased back into the shadows of my mind where innocence and enthusiasm wallowed endlessly for preeminence and understanding. I did, however, spend an inordinate amount of time, on those lazy Sunday afternoons debating the exact form my ministry was to take. I carefully synthesized the various options, each of which vied for a more crystalizing commitment to the focus by which my ministry would be defined.

***

And then the phone rang. That call, in a profound way, launched for me the penetrating inquiry with which I was, for the remainder of my life, destined to deal. The analysis of and my thinking on the subject matter became one of the most emotionally laden topics I was to explore in my revisit. The probing questions were again raised. How could a loving God, the creator and sustainer of life, allow to run rampant, out of control, the destructive and bewildering influences on display at every juncture of existence. How could He allow to go unchecked the distorted consequences, all the evil, painful, and horrible events through which we humankind go? In seminary I was to learn that the theological term for this question was *theodicy*. The phone call forever altered my understanding of God. The spiritual issues that were raised that day haunt me because of the mysterious seeds of understanding that were birthed when I answered the phone call. They grip my soul, not to choke out life, but to send me time after time on a journey in search of spiritual understanding.

Theodicy

Most of us, with a halfway normal brain (notice I said halfway) occasionally have some sort of memory flash that takes us suddenly, without explanation, back to a place, perhaps even to an exact time in space. It is like peering through a looking glass. We do not know what triggered the trance, what gives the location prominence out of a million potential memory locations, but we find ourselves there with some frequency. For me, that mental image usually takes place from a point of reference upward and stepped-back from the particular spot to which I have been escorted. Many times, I suddenly become aware that I am looking down on the bedroom of our apartment in Nashville, Tennessee.

The faded, mauve colored bed covering and the transparent and dusty curtains that hung shapelessly on the double window are not where my mind's eye lands; nor is it the vision of other apartment scenes. The small living room with one of the two apartment entryways is out of focus. The small, seventeen inch, black and white television, wrapped in an ugly green trim, is missing. The small bathroom with pink tile and plastic curtains is forgotten. The kitchen table lodged against the wall with only two chairs is crossed out, stricken through. It is the black phone on which my mind falls. The reason is clear. That call, on that particular day, was to more fully introduce an issue that was to journey alongside me, usually in front of me, for the next fifty years—and even longer.

Chapter 20

Bob Godfrey Died Yesterday

And we know that for those who love God all things work together for good, for those who are called according to his purpose (Rom 8:28).

What then shall we say to these things? If God is for us, who can be against us? He who did not spare his own Son but gave him up for us all, how will he not also with him graciously give us all things. Who shall bring any charge against God's elect? It is God who justifies. Who is to condemn? Christ Jesus the one who died—more than that, who was raised—who is at the right hand of God, who is indeed interceding for us. Who shall separate us from the love of Christ? Shall tribulation, or distress, or persecution, or famine, or nakedness, or danger, or sword? As it is written, 'For your sake, we are being killed all the day long; we are regarded as sheep to be slaughtered.' No, in all these things we are more than conquerors through him who loved us. For I am sure that neither death nor life, nor angels nor rulers, nor things present nor things to come, nor powers, nor height nor depth, nor anything else in all creation will be able to separate us from the love of God in Christ Jesus our Lord (Rom 8:31–39).

THE PHONE RANG. WITH less than excitement, I offered, "Hello." My mother, not bothering with the customary response, mournfully whispered, "Bob Godfrey died yesterday." She went on to say, "They discovered his body on a lonely mountain road with four bullets lodged in his head." Her words echoed in my head—Bob Godfrey died yesterday. Bob Godfrey died yesterday. For some unknown reason, I was not shocked. Numbness replaced a long silence as she said again, "Bob Godfrey died yesterday."

At that moment, I was confronted with the harsh reality that one of the most noble influences on my life was gone at the tender age of thirty-four. My mind was consumed with the refrain: Bob Godfrey died yesterday. In a crystalizing rationalization, Bob Godfrey was but a name among a million names. He represented a temporary headline. This news was much like the quip from Mark Twain when he said, "When you die, the world will admire you for an hour and forget you forever."[1] Twain's retort shadows the realities of life and death. Bob Godfrey was to a wife and a child a broken and lifeless image, a vanishing love who had once laughed and cried with them. To his parents, his death was the tragedy they feared—the foreboding instrument that had pricked the bubble of parental anxiety. To me, it was the loss of a friend whose influence I could never lay down.

Was he not someone to every man? Did his untimely end not represent those events and tragedies of life that leave us emotionally and spiritually drained, sometimes hopeless? In ministry, we face the confusion of it all with uninvited regularity. Bob Godfrey's earthly end represented the evil and suffering with which all of humankind is called to deal. Shakespeare so poignantly and painfully wrote of it in his unforgettable play, *Macbeth*.

> Life's but a walking shadow, a poor player,
> That struts and frets his hour upon the stage,
> And then is heard no more. It is a tale
> Told by an idiot, full of sound and fury,
> Signifying nothing.[2]

As believers, we are quick to voice disagreement with the playwright. We choose, rather, to remember that through Christ not all hope is gone. Through God's grace, all are valued, loved, and forgiven. While we stand back to debate the sad and storied existentialism of Shakespeare, the *Bob Godfrey moments* still exist to shake our faith to the sinew of our souls. None of us can fully understand how God would allow such a senseless murder. It is also inconceivable that God would allow the newborn child to die in her crib at night. Each of us can scold the pathos of our own lists of

---

1. Neider, ed., *Autobiography of Mark Twain*. Actually, I picked up the quote from Todd Fisher, my former pastor in Shawnee, Oklahoma.
2. Shakespeare, *Macbeth*, Act 2, scene II.

Gift Revisited

why. Far too often our search for understanding comes crashing into our meaningful world. Answers are short-lived. The search for them is painful, and it can take our breath away. Our pain, our confusion, our longing for meaning gives witness to a tragic snuffing out of light. Hundreds and hundreds of Bob Godfrey events continue to happen, most of which may not flatten our faith, but they do wrinkle the parchments on which God's plan for us is written.

A poignant thought captures my attention as I write this fifty year old story. Yesterday was the twenty-fifth anniversary of the bombing of the Alfred P. Murrah Federal Building in Oklahoma City, Oklahoma. I was there. Yes, I remember where I was. I remember the emotions that swelled in massive crescendo on that day and the ones following that event. As the great evangelist Billy Graham preached a few days later in that very city, "A lot of faithful, God-fearing people are asking the question, why? How could God allow evil to inflict such a dastardly blow?"[3]

This tragedy was again a replay of the unreconcilable questioning that took place when I heard, almost as if it had just happened, "Bob Godfrey died yesterday." I still, even today, get the vision of the black phone. Who has not cried out, along with the Preacher, "Vanity of Vanities, all is vanity?" (Eccl 1:2). Bob Godfrey kind of events beckon us, time after time, to seek understanding from the compassionate volumes of Scripture's familiar words of comfort: "For we know, that for those who love God all things work together for good, for those who are called according to his purpose" (Rom 8:28). We are then compelled to read further: "What then shall we say to these things? If God is for us, who can be against us? He who did not spare his own Son but gave him up for us all, how will he not also with him graciously give us all things" (Rom 8:31, 32).

I must confess, as Dr. Graham did more than twenty-five years ago in Oklahoma City, I too am compelled to acknowledge that I have no glamorous and resolute answers—at least none that come neatly bundled in some shiny package of universal understanding. What I will do is offer some things I have learned in the many years since that Bob Godfrey moment—the experiences that launched me on a personal journey in quest of a deeper and more promising understanding. Ultimately, each person must find ways by which to process his experiences: listening to counsel, seeking

---

3. Most major television networks provided live coverage of the service on Sunday, April 23, 1995.

understanding from trusted advisors and, most of all, holding conversation often and honestly with the loving Father.

***

The quest for complete knowledge has provided me not answers but options, more meaningful degrees of grace and insight. Over the years, I have delivered many funeral messages, conducted numerous counseling sessions, and more than anything, provided for many wounded souls a shoulder on which to cry. Hopefully, some have been blessed by insights I have shared, thoughts through which some degree of light might have fallen. A few family members who attended one of those funeral services have occasionally dropped by to offer appreciation—most have moved on. Generally, those who have shown appreciation do so not because of the wisdom of my counsel but because of my willingness to listen and to be nearby, a fellow struggler who walked along with them on the path of anguish, who shared hurt and the quiet confidence of *God in us*.

I received few new and life-altering insights from the writer/preacher John Claypool, but what his writings did do for me was to pry open a little farther the door that stood between my meager grasp of knowledge and his perception of ultimate truth. I owe much to Claypool's thoughts and expressions, and herein officially acknowledge his mind and heart behind much that follows. I am immensely indebted to him for the way he helped parse the assumptions of my thinking and how he helped bring a deeper and more vibrant awareness for truth. It is his story and the way he told it that, to a large degree, exposed me to a deeper understanding of the many Bob Godfrey moments in my life.[4]

In 1978, during my very first week as lead pastor, word came that the twelve-year old daughter of one of our most supportive families had been struck by a truck. A few hours later, I stood with the mother by the bedside of the girl as the doctor unplugged the ventilator that had kept her alive long enough for friends and family to arrive. She was gone in seconds. Another black phone moment was happening. During that little girl's funeral, I turned to John Claypool's book, *Tracks of a Fellow Struggler*. The book is comprised of the four sermons he preached surrounding the death of his ten-year old daughter. She was a victim of leukemia. In the book, as he did from the pulpit, he addresses the experiences of that horrific event. In his

---

4. Claypool, *Tracks of a Fellow Struggler*.

book, Claypool invites his readers to journey with him through the diagnosis, the anguish, and the suffering. Finally, he allows them to experience with him, his family, and his congregation the process of acceptance and recovery.

I think that book is out of print, although when I mentioned it to my pastor in Shawnee, Oklahoma, he was able to find a copy for a mother whose very young son had just died. Our church had been praying for his recovery for weeks and weeks, but all too soon he was gone, leaving the family totally devastated. Sometime later, my pastor told me that the mother had, after many months of counseling, found a Godly element of peace, even some understanding, through the reading of *Tracks of a Fellow Struggler*.

***

Romans 8:28 is a wonderful verse. We turn to it with frequency when those mysterious, unexplained moments of fear and uncertainly crash into the depth of our existence. These words have been of enormous comfort for the hurting. They have unbelievable power to draft an element of hope for the bewilderments of life. Sometimes, however, we can get the feeling that the story is not being fully exposed. In our deepest despair we may want to cry out, "Is there not more; has not something been left out?" At those times, scripture does offer hope: "And we know that for those who love God all things work together for good, for those who are called according to his purpose" (Rom 8:28).

I have found myself frequently wondering if something has been omitted from this verse—something overtly obscure. Guilt usually reminds me that my narrowminded scrutiny is misguided. When evil seems to win and babies die in the crib at night, our mindset is rightfully at a different place. Questions recur. Do all things really work out? Paul's words do not seem to reveal the exact answers for which we so desperately search. Let us admit it; most of us have been there. Truth is, many things do not work out, at least in this life. Pains diminish, but never completely leave us. Pain management seems today to be the buzzword, not pain relief.

Let us take another fearful step—evil seems to win more often than we think it should. The elderly wait, without voice, with soiled beds and poor healthcare, while nursing home officials, at least some of them, never miss a meal or fail to take a luxurious vacation. The poor and homeless are not written off as completely worthless, but as hopeless, mentally ill, drug and alcohol abusers with not enough ambition to change their clothes or to find one of the abundant jobs at McDonalds. Could there be something left out? Thousands of Bob Godfreys die every day. Tennyson puts it well:

> The woods decay, the woods decay and fall,
> The vapors weep their burden to the ground,
> Man comes and tills the field and lies beneath,
> And after many summers dies the swan.[5]

We must still come to admit, however, our tendency to point a finger at Romans 8:28 and say that Paul was a little short sighted and misguided. In reality, this verse was not written to offer explanation or to provide divine insight into life's mysteries. It is a simple affirmation that God is in charge and that he can and will help bring measured resolution to the deepest wounds imaginable.

***

If this is true, how then do we as believers reconcile that the pain and suffering from life's deepest and most tragic events can be allowed when the holiest of gods, the only true God, has power to prevent, even eliminate, these things? Many assume that the right and proper solution is to accept the inevitabilities of life, more carefully monitor and control our emotions, and "take it like a man." We must never forget that God knows best and that his ways are not our ways. We take it one step farther and reason that we must not question God. He knows best and he will work things out if we just pray long enough and hard enough. To question God, as this reasoning suggests, borders, in my line of reasoning, near the gate of sinful assumption. It smacks of disobedience, nearly treason. This is an option that Claypool calls *the road to unquestioning resignation*.[6]

Claypool knew that this road would not provide the ultimate answers for his anguish. He knew that this journey does not resonate in cadence with the broken, confused, and bewildered soul. We too have discovered this truth. We understand and accept that God is in charge, but we also feel that his rule can become clouded and misunderstood, perhaps even distorted, when the painful experiences of life suddenly and without apology

---

5. Tennyson, *Tithonus*.
6. Claypool, *Tracks of a Fellow Struggler*.

step in. To ask why, even to demand answers from God, has its own therapeutic import. Jesus prayed in the garden, "My God, my God, why hast thou forgotten me?" (Matt 27:46, KJV).

The God/Man knew that the anguish of a broken spirit hungers for answers to its deepest longings and pains. It is important to remember that implicit in the asking is also the faith that light can break on our troubled spirits. God is not offended when we ask him for answers. He recognizes it is to him that our trust is fully given. By placing him on the center stage of our pain, we bear witness that our life stands in him and in him alone.

Our verse does not say all things are good. Nor should it. There is much in life that is mystery. To probe more deeply into the *why* of divine instruction is a part of the human spirit with which God has gifted us. To question God may not totally be the egregious sin that many envision it to be. After the death of Claypool's daughter, he was inundated by hundreds of expressions of encouragement. Although much appreciated, most came woefully short of comfort. Only one word that allowed John Claypool a sliver of light came from his friend Carlyle Marney, who offered, "You know John, I sometimes feel that God does owe us an explanation." It was not the seemingly divine obscurity of the comment that stirred Claypool's soul, that brought the light of hope. It was the realization that God loves and understands humankind in ways unexplainable, that he was and is the "very present hope in times of all trouble" (Ps 41:6).

***

Sometimes we think we can, on our own, find adequate reprieve and sufficient answers to life's tragedies. To help solve life's mysteries, many employ the most modern analytical absurdities imaginable. However, to walk the way to total and complete intellectual understanding is not the most desirable path. Many disagree with this statement. In fact, they argue that it is best to yield to life's absurdities and to accept that one is never to experience ultimate meaning and understanding. They argue that mankind is hopelessly adrift, destined to plunge, at any moment, into an abyss of desolation, void of meaning and understanding.

Even believers can painfully settle into this way of thinking. We may call it "living with fate," the rationalization that the imperfections and misappropriations of the universe are conditions inherent in a creation void of any divine influences. It is callously argued that God is the great clockmaker.

He wound up the clock. He is now waiting, just out of reach, allowing the clock to unwind, with no alteration to his original design.[7] Moreover, the non-believer must resign himself to the inevitabilities of an existence void of any transcendence. He does not allow that God, if there is one, interacts with his creation in any tangible, demonstrative way. Many literary voices, during the days when this document was originally penned, echoed some of these same thoughts concerning the futilities and mysteries of our existence. Earnest Hemingway provides a classic example in *A Farewell to Arms* when Catherine, one of the central characters in his novel, observes, from the perspective of her tragic and depressing existence, that "life is just a dirty trick."[8] Camus, in his short, insightful rendering *The Stranger*, concludes that the crime that led his central character to the gallows was not the crime of murder; it was not crying at his mother's funeral.[9] The absurdity in this way of thinking is further to be isolated in the writing of Jean-Paul Sartre in his theatrical production, *No Exit*.[10] The theme, within itself, gives birth to the ultimate despair to which he is alluding—that there are no answers to life's deepest questions.

This kind of *when God is silent* thinking leaves us thirsting for genuine hope void of any *God in us* awareness. There is no denying that good as well as evil is ever present. Evil and tragic events do happen. Disappointments and heartaches abound. Who could deny it? But who could deny the good that rises out of the ashes of despair like the proverbial Phoenix, exhibiting both hope and meaning? "Life is essentially a series of events to be born and lived through, rather than an intellectual riddle to be played and solved."[11]

***

Up to this point, we can agree on some things. With a degree of certainty, we have identified the existence of an abundance of *Bob Godfrey* moments. Next, we have found no easy way by which to find personal exemption from the pain, confusion, and doubt or even satisfactory release

---

7. For more explanation of this theory, check the article by Schwartz, "Watchmaker Analogy."
8. Ernest Hemingway, *A Farewell to Arms*, 283.
9. Camus, *The Stranger*.
10. Sartre, *No Exit*.
11. Claypool, *Tracks of a Fellow Struggler*.

from the hopelessness they bring. We have acknowledged that some attempts to lessen the anguish may fall distressfully short.

Before any additional despair sets in, we need to turn again to Romans 8:28. I am reminded once more that the verse makes no claim that all things are good. There is, however, an element of the final, *not-yet* moment inherent in the verse. There is the realization that ultimately God has the final say. This is the "God ain't done with you yet" kind of awareness you want when life's tragic moments become very personal. What we have here is a microcosm of God's nature and evidence of God's plan and purpose; the good over evil teaching is visibly on display. For those who are in relationship with the Creator, this promise is most real. The promise of this verse is especially of comfort to those who love the Lord. It is not that those outside the relationship do not have some level of assurance, for they do. It is that those of us who are in this love-forgiveness relationship can more easily and naturally access the benefits and hope resulting from our intimate relationship with God.

A literal translation of this *God-man relationship* is defined by the verb that is used. It reads "God co-operates with us." We may not fully understand or even want to accept the harshness of the moment, but an awareness of God working alongside is an encouragement for our weariness, for our hurt, for our pain. God is not just walking a mile in our shoes; he is tugging us along and helping us to trust more in his love and to be consumed less by our painful and perplexing circumstances.

A quest for knowledge and our passion for meaningful answers to the distress is not an affront to our faith. It is a product of our human sense of curiosity. A begging for understanding is another. We want answers to life's most confounded questions, and we feel we deserve them. We often forget that full and complete understanding cannot be ours in any light of immediacy. The story of Adam and Eve sheds a revealing light on this human pathos: "God spread the whole of creation out before Adam and Eve like a banquet table and invited them to participate in it fully, to eat, drink, work, multiply; live passionately. But instead of immersing themselves in life, they turned rather to the tree of knowledge of good and evil, the symbol of the ultimate experience of all things that belong to God alone and lusted after it."[12] Our partnership with God, his co-operating with us, is a knitting to-

---

12. Claypool. The origin of this quote is not identified in my 1976 writing, but I assume it to be from *Tracks of a Fellow Struggler*.

gether of his will with our desire for understanding. Now, we know "in part and then we shall . . ." (1 Cor 13: 9).

There is increasing hope along this journey of our *not-now* moments. God provides many helps along the way. Simply accepting that the full drama may not yet have been written can bring a renewed level of expectancy. It is like the proverbial iceberg. What we see on the surface may provide only some inkling of the volumes of grace yet to be revealed. Perhaps, more than anything else, we must not forget who God is. Even more importantly, we must remember *Who* God is to us. He cares deeply about his creation. He experiences sorrow when man is out of step with his divine purpose. He understands how we feel when our world is turned upside down. He grieves over the ills of a broken creation and genuinely cares when his order folds into disorder. He who knows the robin's fall stands beside us. He cooperates with us on every turn, erasing the darkness of defeat and despair. He wipes the tears from the broken spirit and the wounded heart. Jesus did not show heartbreak just over Jerusalem (Luke 19:41–44); his compassion covers the expanses of creation.

Imagine, if you will, the swelling emotion of the disciples when Jesus calmed the raging sea: "What manner of man is this, they cry, that even the wind and the waves obey His voice?" (Mark 4:35–41). The damaged soul needs calming. The raging cosmos too is damaged and in need of healing. In so many ways, the world is out of step. God longs to work with his creation, to bring order out of disorder, grace out of greed, and harmony to the misguided spirit.

I want to offer one concluding thought. Each person could possibly draft his own list of ways by which to calm the raging Bob Godfrey storms. I have worked, to some extent, on that list in this writing. Mostly, I feel compelled to turn again to John Claypool, whose anguish over the death of his ten-year-old daughter was a churning cauldron of distressed emotions. As earlier noted, Claypool got a lot of advice on ways to cope with his loss. Nowhere in his grief experience did he belittle the reasoning of his friends and congregation. The inadequacy of that counsel was not adjudged, nor was it ignored. All of it held some degree of importance. He did, however, through a deep exploration of the soul, come to realize that no answer was adequate, no instruction able to completely define and calm his brokenness.

At Claypool's deep hours of despair, he began to hear the soft whisper of grace. Light, though faint and questionable, was breaking. It was, I suppose, a Godly message of "it does take time . . . ," but yet, it put Claypool on a road, as he described it, more promising to travel. The road of *we must not question God* was far too rough; a journey for nothingness and the unavailability of meaning was too short-lived, forever flawed. God whispered to John Claypool, "remember gratitude."

The movie projector began to reverse the film. The question was replayed before his mind. Ten years of joy with his beautiful Laura Lue began to unfold in Claypool's mind. Remembering all those precious moments infused Claypool and his family with a profound reassurance, one with promise. Gratitude for those years seemed to be the only emotion that brought some moments of comfort and promise, some slow release from the anguish and distress. He was forced to deal with a question, be it so simple and kind: Would he choose to have been the beneficiary of those experiences, to have embraced the utter joy of a precious life of tender promise or would he not? His choice was clear. His answer simple. Yes! His gratitude for the ten years was only the beginning of acceptance, of understanding, but it was a good beginning. Pain did not suddenly slip away. There was no snuffing out the flame of burning anguish, but a new peace and renewed partnership with his Lord appeared. There was a glimmer of promise. Claypool had discovered that the emotion of gratitude was the surest path to meaningful recovery.

May God give all of us his grace to show our gratitude to him who is the giver and sustainer of life and to him all glory be given both now and forevermore. Amen.

Chapter 21

Reflections from the Past

DURING OUR FIRST PHONE conversation, I hoped to convince Jack that my darting in and out of the ecclesiastical world yielded adequate evidence that I had, in identifiable ways, mended a few of the shattered dreams and broken promises resident in humankind. I hoped he would recognize I had not fallen victim to the temptations of a world gone amuck, had not unnecessarily compromised my faith perspective, and had, in fact, successfully flicked a few coins into the coffers of a floundering humanity.

It was important to me that the image he identified was one of a thriving and accomplished servant of God. With some carefully chosen words, my efforts to define and defend my success rang promising, and my objectives yielded some level of contentment. However, the memories of my failures, the lingering guilt and the crippling residue from my exit from pastoral ministry still lingered like some cloud of despair.

Although Jack did not know it, our conversation dredged to the surface multiple missteps, discouraging displays of pride, and intrusive remorse. The questions that I needed to address in a more profound and restorative way suddenly appeared: How can I make right, in any demonstrative way, the misappropriation of my life. A revisit was soon to appear, and the substance of that appearance brought new hope and began some long-needed repair to the broken spirit with which I had lived for too many years.

My revisit began with a fresh awareness that my life was at one time honest and open to the God of creation and that the surrender of my will to his was not insincere and fragmented. It confirmed that the alterations to my life over the past fifty years needed careful consideration. More than anything, I needed to taste again the joy of my relationship with a loving and gracious God. It proved to be a revisit of incalculable joy. I learned that remorse can be lessened through a journey back to Bethel. The adventure was at first slow, but the ultimate destiny was unimaginably rewarding. A revisit can do the same for you. Rewriting the original sermons, the exploration of inalterable truth, moved me beyond the staleness in my life, defused the hopelessness that was holding me motionless. The revisit was an answer, one beyond the realms of human understanding.

An accelerating awareness of forgiveness, a lifting of darkness, the lessening of shame and regret appeared in vivid radiance. The instruction to rewrite the messages of old was, to me, an authentic signature from God. It reassured me that my life had not been wasted, that my usefulness and value were not only viable but held the potential for an even greater influence. I was destined to find meaning not just for myself but for those on whom I had inflicted distress. During my revisit to the old folder of sermons, no new philosophies or theological argument awaited discovery. The fundamentals of my faith had shifted very little. But now, in one infinitesimal moment, I was granted an audience with the quiet and sure voice of God.

I did not recognize the manuscripts as illustrations of my brilliance nor as some mystic texts for a symposium on universal knowledge and understanding. I simply viewed them as an autograph of my faith, directing me to a life that was to be lived in surrender to the majesty and authority of God. I was suddenly on a journey, a wonderous excursion designed to repair the inadequacies of vanishing productivity to which I had grown accustomed. It was a purging of the spirit, a coming to terms with inconsistencies and the misguided direction that had served, too often, to define my work in the Church. It was a compelling invitation to explore the pleasures and vitalities of my faith, to renew the joy and sustaining gift of God's forgiveness and grace, and to reconsider the meaning and purpose to which I had been called many years before.

Reading through a few of my old sermons did not provide a sudden mystical understanding of my moments of darkness and struggle, nor did it bring precise clarity to those moments when I had doubted myself, doubted God. My exposure to these writings was a poignant reconnection to divine grace. It was reinvigorating and restorative; it was a catharsis, a progression of memories that brought renewed awareness that life always has ultimate meaning, regardless of circumstances and the pathos of the day-to-day.

This process brought release to the mundane and shapeless calculations that had burdened my life with a disconcerting familiarity.

A revisit can unleash moments of shame that may have faded to some extent over the years, faded, but never completely released their piercing and intrusive influence. A new awareness of the perpetuality of forgiveness can suddenly appear. The excursion can invite new discoveries, establish vistas of promise, help revive forgotten joys. It can replace bitterness and the malcontent of spirit. Even though time may continue to race on with shrill and dissonant fury, major adjustments and a resurgence of reasoning stand ready, able to replenish a diminished sense of purpose.

A revisit will never completely erase the anxiety and reflections of distress with which we have struggled for what may seem to us a lifetime, but it will mark a sustaining place of renewal, a fresh and promising new point of origin. It will not allow us to start again, but it will raise our heads and our hearts a little higher, elevate our spiritual confidence beyond the influences of pride and self-love, and establish a more promising course, a new road to travel with new possibilities on which to fix our sights.

In my revisit, the sacred Word of God was enlivened. Reflections, good but also somewhat disconcerting, were once again vivid and concentric. I recalled, with clarity, moments when God was mercifully real to me. I also easily recognized times when his presence had been blighted by disparaging thoughts and rebellion. Blatant miscalculations still flashed with vivid exactness, but now they ceased to be an intrusive and bewildering distraction. To be sure, there is some inherent risk in a revisit. An infusion of painful reflections and the recounting of regrets may come mercilessly flooding back. For certain, darkness and defeat command more than a caviler reflection or two, more than some elaborate attitude adjustment. When we are earnest and sincere, we will recognize, in a profound way, the presence of a loving Father who can ease the invisible pain and manage in a benevolent manner the perpetual wasting away of our souls. If we allow the revisit to do so, the Holy Spirit of God will reaffirm and then perfect his forgiveness, allowing for the continuance of the ministry to which we have been called.

For most, these magical times of replenishment and renewal may be singular, at best rare and unexpected. We can discover that the terrain on which we once traveled, those experiences of significant and lasting purpose, may not be as parched and dried as we once imagined. We may be surprised to see life in them again, to discover the value they once provided and know again the scent of the familiar, the fragrance of meaningful passion. We might discover that the good pleasures of our ministry are still resident, that they have survived the passing of idle time and the staleness of our belaboring work. We may find that our efforts, those seemingly rendered nearly worthless by the crisscrossing of desert travel and the dry and lifeless day-to-day, have actually shown a modest element of productivity and marginally thrived, though our efforts may have been feeble and unimpressive.

A revisit can suddenly show itself, especially during those times when aspirations and hopefulness are nearing extinction, when we are desperately thirsty to discover the authentic joy of our faith just one more time. A revisit can bring the transformation of those dwindling times when we furiously grasp for any remaining thread with which to weave some tapestry of productive service. I understood that my revisit held no invitation to preach again, but I was consumed by the desire to suspend remorse, to dissuade regret and failure, to replace my wounded ego with something pure and promising. I was not to preach again, but to write, to tell my story, not with bewilderment and despair, but with renewed instruction, to be honest with God and with myself.

Awakening from my despondency did not release to me again the gift of preaching, but the memories of that giftedness were strong and vibrant, warm and familiar. Old disciplines of faith were not resurrected, only refreshed. My revisit broke that cloud of despair and diminishing hope in which I had been imprisoned for fifty years. It was reassuring to recognize that my faith journey had not been completely ill-spent.

Going back to Bethel can do the same for any who desire a fresh understanding of the misshapen reflections of how it used to be, never pausing to reach the unfathomable *how it can and should be*. Your revisit may not, in the least of ways, resemble mine, but your journey will find its own unique and sustaining purpose. It can renew vanquished dreams and replenish a lingering, possibly abandoned hope. Only you can discover the best road on which to travel.

Chapter 22

The Mystery of Restoration

MY THIRST FOR SUCCESS had often coddled the echoing sounds of disillusionment and unwittingly invited an unpleasant and sordid acceptance of the destiny to which I seemed to be assigned. To be sure, when the call from Jack arrived, I was floundering aimlessly. Church ministry was little more than an image, suspended and distant on an eroding hillside of exasperating chance. I appeared to be poised, ready to plunge head-first into the capricious and inarticulate chasms of despair. I viewed truth with an element of caution. The passing of years and my newly emerging attention to political rhetoric had begun to marginalize clear and reasonable thinking. Happiness was only an illusion; meaning and any aspirations for productive ministry were now hopelessly lodged in a bewildering and onerous submission to the inevitable.

In each of the six manuscripts contained in this book, the themes have not strayed far from my original thinking. Topics of importance are not slashed and dissected. The subject matter was extremely important to me fifty years ago, and now, through these six newly framed writings, I have attempted to capture a compendium of my thinking and to more clearly articulate my understanding of the God into whose service I have been called. However, and I do not apologize for it, some twists and turns should be apparent to you. I often make a reference to current events and entangling circumstances.

Today's news has not been ignored or displaced by antidotal sensationalisms. I feel lead to address some piercingly critical topics. In the new stenographic renderings, old words have been replaced by new ones, not that they were lacking in value or had been altered to appease the congregation.

Though the essence of the words may have occasionally appeared pale and cloudy, they had never been weakened or compromised during my years of wandering. They were always standing nearby to provide some glimmer of promise, the anticipation of a better tomorrow.

In the essay to be found in the next chapter, my thinking has not shifted away from my original understanding of truth, but it has been tightened and, to some extent, influenced by the political discord currently running out of control in this nation. The opinions may in the end be singularly mine, but the invitation to search and pray for truth comes from God. To read the old sermons again brought new resolution to a faith that I had allowed to ease away from the center of my life, permitting it to fade from sight. I heard the council of Helmut Thielicke again, words that I granted only a polite and insincere place of agreement at the original writing, but now provided the perspective from which my fellow *ecclesaholics* and I can find repose: "Use the time, which may perhaps be short, to practice love wherever you can, to be a joyful flowing fountain in the midst of the desert of paralysis, hopelessness, and sullen disillusionment. And be humble rendering your own false and romantic plans for your life to his mysterious fatherly will."[1]

***

In discovering those old sermon manuscripts, I was exposed to events and circumstances where both the philosophy and the understanding of my faith, the theology by which I was adjudged, stood on level ground, clear and certain, unchangeable and authentic. Fifty years ago, social, even political influences held some place of interest, but reflected only a transitory value toward shaping my views as to where a Christian should comfortably stand regarding the relevancy of the current, disconcerting, and overly analyzed issues found in the newspaper.

My revisit shifted my perspective. Although the separation of church and state remained in proper perspective, a renewed enthusiasm and passion had already, with the presidential election within sight, began to emerge. The soon to follow essay on civil obedience awaited updating and, by nature of existing political and theological controversy, needed to more accurately define the issues and dynamics of faith with which we, as

---

1. Thielicke, *Life Can Begin Again*, 193.

believers, struggle: racial injustice and the beleaguering influences of the political world.

Chapter 23

Living with the Rights We Have
A Call for Civil Obedience

HISTORY REPEATS ITSELF! Is that a crazy statement or what? As far as I can see, the expression is a grandiose oxymoron that makes those who utter it look wise, maybe more profound, but it may also reveal that we are out of touch with reality. What is happening today has never happened before. We can, however, identify experiences of today that do have a stark resemblance to past events. From our purposeful scrutiny, we might glean insight or learn invaluable lessons, yet we cannot relive what has gone before. The hopeful news is that we perhaps have a better chance to "get it right this time around" in relation to many of those happenings to which we append "history repeats itself." Unfortunately, the characteristic of the events that commonly earn that epithet is that they have usually been hurtful, even destructive, in nature. Most have left irreparable scars on society.

In my many years, I have experienced a multitude of history-making events, ranging from the assassinations of John F. Kennedy, Bobby Kennedy, and Martin Luther King Jr. to the coronavirus pandemic of 2020. The brutal "caught-on-camera" death of African American George Floyd, at the hands of four Minnesota police officers, now finds its own place on my list of history repeating itself happenings. The alterations, adjustments, or even changes we make in reaction to his death and to similar events become for society a critical test of the moral and ethical compasses that in the past have successfully guided us into a more promising future.

Historically, we have made many changes in our treatment of our fellowman, and yet, the underlying causes of hatred and injustice have

Living with the Rights We Have

remained intact. Analysis of the underlying reason is simple at this point; it can easily be identified. We Christians call it *sin*. It runs the gamut of all history—pride to prejudice, man's inhumanity to man in its various and sundry shapes and sizes. At this fork in the road, a self-lecture for me is mandatory. I need to be reminded that we Americans, as a society, have made enormous strides forward regarding hate, racism, and other debilitating crimes. We should, however, remember the truth, the whole truth, regarding the injustices we have inflicted on each other. I do not think we will necessarily learn new things from the George Floyd tragedy, but we should be challenged to renew and improve our efforts at promoting equality and harmony among every citizen of this great country. Improvements will continue to come. Changes will be made. Some semblances of peace can be gathered from the debris of our faulty and sinful actions.

As believers, as a society, we must smack ourselves on the wrists. Judicial and legislative improvements are always on trial and must be enacted expeditiously and with determination. There is always a place for change, change that will lead to the betterment of the oppressed and disenfranchised. At the moment, current events stand poised between two critical questions. First, are we applying lessons learned from hauntingly similar events, and second, and far more critical, are we consciously envisioning ways to make the changes necessary to demonstrate lessons have been learned?

Does history really repeat itself? The Achilles heel of society is that we keep making the same dumb mistakes. We have, thanks to a decent distribution of brain power, learned better and more creative ways to attempt resolution. Although we continue to say we make improvements, often only directives designed to appease the far right or the far left are drafted, resulting in advancements that are meager or ineffective.

The Bible reminds that time will slowly but steadily give witness to a polarization of good and evil. In no way am I suggesting that lethargy should rule and that efforts to pour time, energy, and money into judicial reformation are wasted. If nothing else, these labors are necessary to sustain civilization and to preserve civil dignity! We must continue to have a voice and be actively engaged in change and equality for everyone. Jesus would have us do no less. I am not attempting to be apocalyptic, but before losing my audience, I must unequivocally pronounce that, in the end, victory is assured. Evil will not win. The consummation of history will be clearly defined by the historic and conquering return of the Prince of Peace. All rule that Satan may have will be snuffed out. Evil will be cast into the lake of fire and then victory will be complete.

If nothing else, we get a small taste of hope when we remember this truth. Every effort we make to right the wrongs of our prejudices are consistent with our Lord's ultimate victory over sin. Why does this matter? Above all, it is an encouragement that this *until then* awareness should sustain and motivate us to work while the day is young, for the darkness comes. Our job is to ward off and to stand against the darkness as long as he (Jesus) tarries and history rushes to culmination. More than anything else, it is in obedience to that greatest of all commandments—the *go ye* that challenges and empowers us to invite any and every man to the banquet of God's saving and sustaining grace.

Edmund A. Steimle, former professor at New York City's Union Theological Seminary, marginally stressed a few of the young "preacher boy" students the day he spoke during a class at Southern Seminary. His text for the lecture was taken from Matthew 25:1–13, the parable of the ten virgins. Steimle provided an explanation of this passage so different to what I had always assumed it to emphasize. I am not sure his words shocked me as much as they disappointed. I clearly remember the mesmerizing impact of his disclosure. I felt some amazement, but mostly embarrassment when I realized my arrow of interpretation had skidded slightly by the target and had missed the most important element in this holy passage. To the best of my memory, I want to paraphrase some of his words.

I know many of you have used this text with some frequency in those weekend revivals. Your main emphasis in preaching has been on the return of the LORD. You have pleaded with fervor, not just in support of the return of Christ, but also on the need to be prepared for the anticipated, returning bridegroom.

The major emphasis in this passage it not that we must be ready for the return of the King; it is more on the activity and service that cannot be minimized or eliminated during the interim until that arrival happens. A careful examination of the context and the time of writing for this passage can be enlightening. The New Testament church had grown increasingly weary. They had expected the LORD to return quickly after his ascension—certainly had anticipated his return during their lifetime. Having based most of their hope on the return of a conquering king, they had begun, in despair, to release that energizing expectation.

Perhaps they had misunderstood the events at Calvary, seeing them only as a temporary setback for Israel's rise to world power and failed to understand that the kingdom ultimately was within the heart of each believer. Maybe they had failed to embrace that the final victory was to be realized through eschatological promise.[1]

I want to move from the words of Steimle back to my own thoughts on this passage. Sadly, the angst of the disciples may display a malady from which, at least part of the time, we humankind now suffer. The New Testament church had based hope and loyalty far too intently on the shallowness of immediacy, the instant reward of power and prominence, and far too little on the loneliness of the Galilean who promised a mansion for the not yet and the possibility of a cross for the present.

Please do not hear me say that to follow Christ has no assurance for the infilling of daily bread, but please also hear me when I offer that to find authentic nourishment in him who is the bread of life, we must not miss that Jesus also warned his overly eager disciples that the reality of a cross loomed ahead for them too. Yes, there is abundant reward in following Christ, value and meaning beyond the imagination. On occasion, despair can set in when we fail to recognize that the absurdities of life can bend our focus away from what we need to favor more what we want. Effort must be made to avoid distorted and faulty perception of the teaching *my grace is sufficient*. This distorted assumption can suddenly retreat into despair, even anger, and can quickly diminish the hope in which we once trusted.

Possibly, Matthew's purpose in recording this parable was not because the church needed further discourse affirming that the return of the conquering King would ultimately take place, that life as it unfolded would find release from the drudgery of the routine and inconsequential. Maybe the writer felt it important to remind the early New Testament Church that the *until then* needed the value of passionate and sustaining activity, that there was, in the meantime, an abundance of activity to be undertaken.

I want to paraphrase one more of Steimle's thoughts: *The early church needed to anticipate the bridegroom's appearance, but they also needed to hold at bay uninvited and bewildering discouragements resident in any potential delay.*[2] At that point, I realized that those who were genuinely sensitive to the impending joy of celebration were also those who had the foresight and

---

1. The words in italics are my paraphrase, rather than a quote, of the content of his lecture.
2. My paraphrase of Steimle.

the resilience to focus more on the *until then* than they did on the ultimate day of celebration.

We mysteriously find satisfaction and reward in the shallowness of our own despair and then furiously design recovery plans. Often, we do not have the energy it takes to overcome the distress of our souls and the habitual and self-designed roadblocks that distract from a productive and vibrant faith that can lead to the inevitable destruction of it. Many are still lodged on the hills of despair, awaiting the joy of a lingering wedding celebration. God may not condemn our emerging lethargy or pronounce anathema on our lack of constancy in our faltering obedience, but we cannot assume he is pleased with them either.

To stand idly back, fearing to fully engage in life based on the assumption that the final word belongs to those who seek to control our destiny with evil purpose and wicked determination is not the assumption by which we should live. The real heroes in this story are recognized because they had, should the bridegroom be delayed, enough oil in their lamps to last. Those chided were the guests whose oil ran out.

Do you remember hearing about a bizarre scene that is publicly enacted every decade or so and is, for certain, not overlooked by media sources? A certain group or two have prophetically identified the exact date, often even the time of day, when the world will come to an end. On the chosen date, they cluster on some remote hilltop and anxiously await to be taken up by the returning conqueror. To most, this dramatization just does not make any sense, although many misguided sects have tried it.

While most chastise or even ridicule these misguided people, secretly I am a little envious of their display of loyalty, for I do share with them a similar level of hopefulness that the God I serve will show himself in a pronouncement against man's injustice to man and, with finality, bring that which is evil to an end. My fear is that while I patiently wait for wrong to be hamstrung, I will forget that Jesus defined righteousness as a perpetual process; though it is poorly enacted by most, it is *our daily bread*. The church is called to be that one clarion call of right living, hour-to-hour, day-to-day, without wavering. History keeps reminding that silence, the absence of some prophetic voice, can be sinfully injurious to a creation that is in need of redemption. Creation itself needs reconciliation. Could environmental legislation be a marginally courageous effort to that end?

Those who gather on their mountaintop of anticipated glory cannot exclusively bear the guilt for their perceived foolishness; the rest of us who fail to live productive and engaging lives in anticipation of coming redemption are also at fault. If we look only for the time of victory, the value and fervor of our current actions are diluted and of limited value. The church must be alive in the *not-yet* moments and movements in history. Never forget that the Lord himself prayed, "Thy kingdom come on earth as it is in heaven" (Matt: 6:10).

Granted, the kingdom we help to construct on this earth pales in comparison to the kingdom yet unrealized. Our feeble but divine efforts, even our repurposing projects, beg for attention. George Floyd's death has reminded me that the church must have a voice in those "history repeats itself" moments. The irony surrounding his death, the guilt of a faltering and morally deprived society, cannot be ignored or glossed over by some timid voice of protest. It must find some rightful place in the life of we who profess that Jesus is Lord.

We cannot allow historic reminders like the death of George Floyd to distress us beyond repair. They come along too often. We must, however, take seriously the truths that confront us and must repent of every sinful action for which we hold any ownership. I am painfully reminded that I have never completely discarded the prejudices of my childhood. I do not like the intrusions. They are a part of how I was built, and as much as I know I should, I have never been able to lay them down completely. My shame is that I remember when a soft drink was ten cents a bottle, but I also vividly remember when my "colored" friends had their own small elementary school across the tracks just over the knoll in Coke Oven Holler.

Even now, I feel that I could almost reach out and release the thick crimson rope that blocked the darkened stairway leading to the local movie house balcony where those same friends were relegated to sit as the projector clicked on for the first Saturday afternoon newsreel. I can see the cigarette smoke rising as it clouded the rays of the projector that, frame by frame, attempted to report on what was happening in a pain-stricken world. Each frame only hinted at the possibility for peace and prosperity for all. No frame seemed to adequately promise equality for those who climbed the darkened stairways, took their seats, and prayed for news that might hint that someday soon, they would be permitted, with their fellow brothers and sisters, to take their seat below.

The reality is that our responses to "history repeats itself" moments cannot focus singularly on the call for resolutions. Equal attention must be given to the cause of the malady. Both need undivided attention. The Bible identifies the ill that has, from the beginning, bred distortion to life. It is called *sin*. Every person bears its scars. No one is exempt from the pain and distress it generates. To be clear, the fall of man has inched its way across all of creation, so much so that nature is equally fallen and will someday also find redemption. Environmental legislation may be, at best, only a band-aid solution, but in my judgement, it must be judiciously attempted to preserve for future generations some of the beauty and utility of the creation God granted to us for preservation.

This observation is, in a way, out of step with the subject. However, it may just be one more acknowledgment that all of God's creation is flawed and needs repaired. This bleak, even depressing, assumption cannot, however, exempt the church from some level of responsibility. The church may, at the least, be called to continue efforts to put our thumb in the dyke until the Lord returns in triumphant, all-inclusive victory.

***

I understand, as a new, "for real" writer, that inherent danger can be experienced in the careless dating of material. Using an *in time* current illustration can lose most of its energy when the text is read just a few years removed from the event, but I take that risk. The emotion by which one is captured too often dies, not just with the passing of time, but because other events come along whose shadows capture yet another new moment in time—depleting the energy of past moments by seizing emotions for their own value. With no second thought, we quickly replace one tragedy, one moment in time, for the next. The tragic death of George Floyd, at the hands of some Minneapolis police officers, is one such event. As I write, a week of intense demonstrations, both peaceful and harmful, have captured most of the news.

Many agree that some progress is to be gained by peaceful demonstration and that any potential setbacks resulting from property destruction, physical retaliation, and looting have been minimized by the fair and necessary acknowledgement by voices on both sides of the argument. Most agree that any acts of out-of-control violence and destruction are part of the problem and not part of the solution. The just pronouncement has been offered by both sides of the debate that first amendment rights should be allowed and that any criminal activities in protest should not be tolerated, and certainly not applauded.

Living with the Rights We Have

I risk using this illustration and its faulty timelessness because it sets the stage for what I determine to be one of the more challenging statements I will make in this book. When I started this writing, I proposed, as mentioned in many other places, to thumb back through some old notes and manuscripts and rewrite a few of the documents with the benefit of time and experience thrown into the new writing. My intent was never to provide commentary on current events. My simple resolve was to update my presentations of timeless truths and to explore those truths with better language and improved insight. To this point, I feel I have accomplished the objective. My original intent was to stay clear of contemporary issues and to rely only on the value of eternal truths on which I focused in the original writings. However, I believe it is important that a Christian voice be heard during moments when it seems that history is repeating itself.

The commonplace is under attack. The question of racism has now again been vividly raised. Is history repeating itself? Have racism and hatred reared an ugly head again? Was its burial, in the last half of the twentieth century, shallower than originally thought? Is it now time for the church to honestly explore what our voice in the matter should be? Will it call for our congregants to take some stand, broadcast some seeds of hope, raise a reluctant but resolute voice, and disclose in our proclamation a word from the Lord? I think so. If we are to learn anything from history, we best remember that silence from the church can often do more harm than good.

My purpose was never to address moral and ethical issues, but the subject of the text to follow pleads for some level of contemporary reaction. "What Rights Do We Have," the sermon in which these words find validation, invites current thinking regarding the church and may just include some challenge as to how we are compelled to react to the George Floyd incident. From the beginning, I assumed that the way I presented the truth, as exposed in each of the old manuscripts, would not necessarily create a reactionary shift in the thinking of my readers. I did hope my words might at least remind us, in a fresh way, how best to hold more tightly to the fundamental axioms on which the church is built. The death of George Floyd compels us to gain important lessons from the tragedy. We must be reminded of how to embrace more passionately every opportunity to participate in causes that are just and noble.

Nothing can repeat itself, but every day we do observe reproductions of times and circumstances that have slipped away. If we note only similarities to the past, I fear that the evil of the present will be viewed only as a picture of the same misgivings. I fear current tragedies are usually written off as "that's just the way things are." Indifference holds hands with evil and prevents any honorable assumptions of responsibility for the present moment. It is critical that the church not forget the message of the familiar adage, "The only thing necessary for the triumph of evil is for good men to do nothing."[3] Every generation has not only its own unique sinfulness, but also its own unique ways by which restorative action is taken.

Historically, most efforts at social or racial equality have revealed only temporary solutions, and as time marches on, the efforts suffer amendment, even repeal. Racism, bigotry, and hatred have not and will not ever be completely eradicated this side of the Parousia, but, if the effort for resolution is not in perpetual forward motion, then God's mandates and plans for equality are irreparably damaged.

George Floyd's death reminds me that we, as a people, are woefully short of perfection; more than anything, it reminds me that even we in the church have stepped, in our efforts to promote brotherhood among the races, too far to the side. It is not a matter of any debate about trending to the left or to the right. I feel confident Jesus is more concerned about people than politics. The reinvigoration of my thinking in each of these six sermon do-overs has brought for me a renewed and profound awareness of the place and time in my life where my faith was vibrant. I had a faith that was embraced by more than a casual interest, a level of awareness that freely acknowledged the sustaining Lordship of the Christ of Galilee. It was not compromised by a debilitating sin, a darkness of the spirit that extracted joy from my life. I sincerely pray that by reading my thoughts, you will find some encouragement, a renewed purpose by which to right the disheveled wanderings of your faith, a refreshing understanding of your place in the ecclesiastical jungle into which God has called each to serve.

---

3. The origin of this familiar quote finds the most plausible evidence in Edmund Burke's letter to Thomas Edmonds, 1770.

Chapter 24

What Rights Do We Have?

"You have heard that it was said, 'An eye for an eye and a tooth for a tooth.' But I say to you, do not resist the one who is evil. But if anyone slaps you on the right cheek, turn to him the other also. And if anyone would sue you and take your tunic, let him have your cloak as well. And if anyone forces you to go one mile, go with him two miles. Give to the one who begs from you, and do not refuse the one who would borrow from you'" (Matt 5:38–42).

IN HIS MONUMENTAL *A Study of History*, Arnold Toynbee points out that the way a society chooses to deal with the barbarian elements in its midst goes a long way in determining whether it will survive or not. How does the best relate to the worst, the human folk to those who are savage in their behavior? This issue finally led to the downfall of the Roman Empire. They lost the power to stem the tide of inhumane and antihuman forces. This question remains the burning issue at any moment in history, including right now. How do we respond to these persons and forces who seem intent on tearing down what we have worked so hard to create?[1]

Normally, an eye for an eye seems to be, as it has in every generation, a very serious concern. This solution still seems popular: respond to evil by giving evil a dose of its own medicine. In the end, however, does this way of relating to an evildoer really solve the problem of evil? Martin Luther King

---

1. Toynbee, *A Study of History*.

Jr. once said that the logical end of *an eye for an eye and a tooth for a tooth* is that everyone winds up blind and toothless.[2]

***

When it comes to this entire matter, we churchmen may be content to meet spiritual instruction at the least acceptable levels. It does not take a brain surgeon to recognize that the problem with which we so desperately deal is the need to get our minds and our hearts in the right place. We need to navigate life in a way that demonstrates we are under the Lordship of one whose influence and authority is much larger and more consistent than anything we might on our own attempt to emulate. We can easily accept the reasoning that revenge and retaliation have no rightful place in the life of the believer. We know experientially the value of a life lived void of reactionary and uncontrolled rage. We can clearly argue that to fight fire with fire can be mean and nasty and we want no part in it. However, when we react to infraction against us by burying our heads in the sand and pretending that we are justified in handling some conflicts with a controlled and righteous anger, we can come up against a hidden obstacle. When our thinking falls victim to this rationalization it becomes much easier and more natural to validate the *eye for an eye* approach. This attitude provides the surest and safest action to ensure we are not unduly taken advantage of and affords a natural and necessary way to defend our honor and our way of life.

When facing any semblance of offense, we must first ask ourselves this question: How does this affect me personally? Gordon Alport recounts an old but tender story in his excellent book, *The Individual and His Religion*. A young and obviously innocent boy was mesmerized as he stared, for the first time, at a cross. His breath was taken from his lungs, yet enough air allowed him to cry out, "What does it all mean? What is it?" The young boy found himself awestruck. He recognized that something of the mysteriously profound loomed in front of him. From one standing nearby, a response followed, "Young man, that is a replica of the cross on which Jesus the Christ was hung." The young innocent child, still not sure as to the accuracy or significance of the words the elder man offered, made his own observation. "Oh," he reverently offered, "I see. It is the 'I' crossed out."[3] He had uncovered, in that one childlike utterance, an eternal truth of the

2. King, *The Autobiography of Martin Luther King Jr.*
3. Alport, *The Individual and his Religion.*

Christian faith—life is best lived when the selfish *I* is stricken through and the selfless character of the living Christ is allowed to reign in one's life.

Most of us usually ask ourselves how this, whatever 'this' is, will affect me. When historic moments like the George Floyd incident, for example, come along, erupt our stale complacency, and rattle our conscience, even the most indifferent, socially and politically, cannot escape the plea for attention such events present. These events can scar, but mostly they can slightly alter our lives, bringing disruptive irritations that challenge our routines. I will argue that the alteration of our thinking can and should be positive, even transformative. Unfortunately, the change will often, assuming the impact of the event digs even slightly into some level of our consciousness, last only short-term. Before we know it, the event will soon transition to a distorted memory concerning which we, with a sigh of relief, conclude, "I am so glad that we have moved on."

We should, although we usually are not, be haunted by the casualness that feeds our indifference—a self-inflicted malady that invites us to look past the ills and injustices that we willingly dismiss as distraction. We seem content to scroll on by the morning news with only momentary pause. We find the news to be irritating, often depressing. It can inform, but usually seems more destined to rob us of our self-absorption, so we flippantly rush on to chase our own dreams for success and prosperity.

We can cry out all we want, ignore the harsh realities of the moment, and dismissively argue until the cows come home that it is someone else's problem. It is my judgement that a severe damage has been inflicted on the church if we conclude silence is our safest and most honorable approach to any or every injustice to which we are exposed. I have some suspicion we have far too many times been complacent; we have overlooked, sweet-talked, or just plain lied to ourselves when we too easily assume that acts of societal wrong have nothing to do with the Church or with us personally.

Regardless of the frequently fabricated message from the politicians and their take on the matter, the assumed accuracy of recollection of some drunken witness or the shattered expectations of the idealists, all of whom suffocate the truth with no second thought, the George Floyd moment in *history repeats itself* is symptomatic of a greater problem we have far too long been comfortable to define not as systemic or endemic but as manageable. How dare we?

If we water the issue down with the argument that all lives matter, we have only lumped the fault into a more collective passion that instantly relegates the Floyd historic moment from the specific ill to a general, collective awareness any good-natured Christian is willing to affirm. Band wagons that meander along are much easier to mount than those that rumble and echo a courageous message for change. It takes far less commitment to slip aboard a glamorous wagon whose harnessed thoroughbreds calmly gallop through our own comfortable worlds than it takes to yield to inspirational teaching in which God can instruct the believer to a more relevant and influential voice.

We must not forget talk is cheap and that actions do speak louder when our surrender of self is under Godly mandate. It is rare indeed when we can find a voice that cannot be quickly silenced by corrupt and bigoted authorities. Seldom do we hear an utterance in contrast to the auditable, distaining sounds that ceremoniously ooze from the lips of respected and charismatic spokespersons whose own collective consciences have been seared by the lust for power and popularity. I sincerely pray that by the time anyone reads this narrative, laws will have been drafted through the necessary legislative channels to replenish for this nation the zeal for fair treatment. I hope that these actions will ensure that long-awaited and necessary changes have been enacted to address systemic racism. not just in America but around the world.

No sensitive and sane American should ignore that we have inherited, through historic mismanagement, an extremely painful, volatile malady that has, for more than one hundred years, muted every authentic voice for racial equality. America's intentions have been honorable, but more often than can be accurately documented, our best efforts at justice have been woefully misguided, even ignored. Racism is still around. I know it because I, as much as I want to, cannot shake it, at least I cannot ignore the fact that it has been tucked away far too long in the shadows of our major cities, the courtrooms and legislative chambers of our United States.

Authentic healing is a challenge, like a flesh wound that ultimately finds the better journey to recovery when the process of healing begins on the inside. Change is slow, but right now as I write, I am more than ever convinced we in the church must not ignore any longer the disadvantaged and socially abused, dismissively denying their pleas for justice and equality. It just might be our moment in time when we bow in contrition and apologize for indifference and for our willing reluctance to get in the middle of things.

What Rights Do We Have?

Congressman John Lewis, now deceased, devoted most of his life to suffering the consequences of good trouble.[4] He, with some regularity, was willing to risk imprisonment if he believed his actions exposed the blatant sin of man's inhumanity to man. He passed from this world to the next with many physical and emotional scars because of his willingness to suffer for the reward of fairness and justice for all.

Many good-natured souls like me have little difficulty aligning with those who suffer the pains of injustice. However, in the end it is the mean and seemingly suspicious side of the argument that will ultimately garner from us some level of acceptance. With a callous disregard for our witness, we will release our momentary enthusiasm, recognizing as we do that the side of the argument on which we have chosen to stand represents an unpopular flavor-of-the-day and makes us look like the action we once took against bigotry is meddling in problems not correctable or even worth the effort.

Off we run with our tails tucked between our legs, bemoaning that we cannot apologize for our first reaction; instead we back off our initial enthusiasm to devote new energy to some other emerging good cause. Shame on me for never finding the resilience to invest my life more completely in the things that matter the most—often failing to find the courage and stamina to utter an authentic voice or to deny compromise.

Had I joined a peace march in my teenage years, I am confident Martin Luther King Jr. would have immediately booted me off his team. I really wanted to take the courageous step, but my enthusiasm was shallow, perhaps too showy. It certainly was not the noble ambition I purported it to be, and my fear of disapproval from my girlfriend's family was adequate argument to dampen my marginal enthusiasm. I soon moved on to a more popular cause—one I now cannot remember. I did, over the years, regret my failure to channel more promising energy toward causes that mattered and less toward the popular and even financially rewarding purposes.

I could, just like I suspect could many readers, come up with a dozen reasons to argue that the George Floyd moment should not be ignored but that it should be kept in perspective. We can find some level of satisfaction, can sleep more comfortably at night, if we raise a modest voice against the establishment and if we demonstrate, at least by word, that the

---

4. John Lewis (February 21, 1940-July 17, 2020) was an American statesman and civil rights leader who served in the United States House of Representatives for Georgia's 5th district from 1987 until his death.

offended from whom fairness has been stripped should be allowed some acknowledgement.

We can preserve some degree of respectability and acceptance if we thoughtfully have arrived at the socially accepted perspective that keeps things civil and offends no one, especially the law-abiding who sit by us in the pew on Sunday morning. The risk of engagement, even for causes that deserve such action, may not, in the end, seem to merit much time and effort. Most battles for righteousness are difficult to wage without assuming that some sacrifice on our part is inevitable.

The church's lack of some passionate voice might just portend an identifiable guilt, maybe an unconfessed sin on our part. It is guilt, not by association, but guilt from the lack of any voice that exposes our impassioned silence. I know, just as I was aware fifty years ago, that the church, we who identify as part of the Body of Christ, are called to be more like the early New Testament Church about whom the jealous Thessalonian Jews argued, "These men who have turned the world upside down have come here also . . . and they are acting against the decrees of Caesar" (Acts 17:6b, 7b).

Silence can easily be defined as sinful and, at times, equally as appalling and as dangerous as apathy. Apathy suggests indifference. Silence, more than apathy, allows the assumption we are on one side or the other while apathy is viewed as "I do not care about the injustice and do not bother me and, for certain, do not drag me into the debate." Silence more naturally positions us on the negative; it places us on the side that openly denies that any injustice exists. When we are silent, our position on matters of injustice or seasons of intolerance has been registered, naturally inviting the naysayers to include us on their side of the equation. Apathy places us there by easy assumption when in fact, silence forfeits any meaningful argument against the injustice or evil.

With some modest effort, most good-natured, peace-loving Christians can somehow find the courage to raise a level of concern, that is, after acknowledging that the problem may not be as bad as the Black Lives Matter proponents protest. Likewise, most will admit that neither can the issue be ceremoniously swept under the rug as if social injustice had vanished like an ugly aberration. Both confessions end up being little more than a faint echo that reverberates down a darkened canyon of discontent, lacking in persuasion and offered with only a reserved timidity.

To be sure, the hair stands up on the backs of our necks when contentious voices suggest we might be going too far by raising a judgmental

What Rights Do We Have?

objection or even a modest voice expressing our apprehension over the existence of racism. Insecure and socially compromising authorities are quick to suggest that Christians need to stand down on our concern for what we perceive, but may not fully understand, as the unfair treatment of people of color. I am all in for the separation of church and state, but nowhere do I read in Holy Scripture that we should remain silent when massive injustice and discrimination still have a solid foot planted in the rich soil of a nation whose founding fathers suffered enormous cost to establish the land of the free and the home of the brave.

Just a few days ago I endured watching, for the first time, the 1988 film *Mississippi Burning*. Endured may be a mild term given the dramatic way in which hatred and indignity are so violently portrayed in the movie, not just by members of the Ku Klux Klan but also by most white citizens in the community in which the movie was set. It was too uncomfortable for me to watch the entire movie in one sitting. I chose to watch it over a two-day period to slightly control my rage for what the move depicted and my own heartbreak that the same hatred is still present today.

The blight today is just more creatively packaged and hidden. The movie, perhaps, although I doubt so, exaggerates a hateful and bigoted racism, especially in the South. It convincingly reveals how this evil moved by legions beyond festering to a blatant disregard for the rights of African Americans. Yes, I will allow that the movie is probably an over-dramatization of discrimination, but I am not sure it exaggerated it by much.

The curtain opens with the senseless murder of three young men, one of whom is black, who had traveled to a small Mississippi town to help African Americans register to vote. The FBI arrives on the scene when the three young volunteers are determined to be missing. The local law-enforcement officials bristle and become belligerent at the accusation any crime against the three has been perpetrated. The authorities, and most other of the whites in town, are up in arms, arguing that they are law-abiding citizens and that colored people would be fine if they just kept their noses out of the white people's business.

It was not until the end of the movie that I fully discovered the more exact and penetrating reason for my distress. The message of *Mississippi Burning* should not, by any believer in a Holy God, be ignored. After some incredibly hard-fought action, justice has been levied legally against most of the guilty characters. The last scene exposes what we ultimately cannot deny. Many of us frequently demonstrate a hidden partnership with bigotry. It is painful to admit that the chickens do come home to roost, and they may even come home to bring some level of judgement against many of us in the Church.

In the movie, the lead FBI agent, after discovering the body of an ordinary citizen who has hanged himself, responds to a fellow agent, who asks, "Why did he do it? He wasn't even in on it. He wasn't even Klan." Mr. Burg, the lead agent replies, "He was guilty. Anyone is guilty who watches this happen and pretends it isn't. He was guilty all right, just as guilty as the fanatic who pulled the trigger; maybe we all are."[5]

Pride is so dangerous when it allows our misguided reasoning to shield us from our own weaknesses and misgivings. We feel personal injury if there is any possible suggestion that maybe we still harbor some ugly prejudice. We need to first repent and then explore ways to make right any damage our past actions may have inflicted, but we also need to pray for a new openness. Two things quickly eroded my protective guard when the George Floyd travesty exploded. First, I recognized in earnest that my own prejudice had not fully left me. Second, I agreed that African Americans are, in fact, suffering injustices, not just from police profiling but for sundry other reasons.

There is no denying that enormous progress has been made, but the sad truth is that I, along with many others, have assumed that our battles for personal fairness, hard-fought in the past, were capable of sustaining progress in the present. The truth is that bigotry did not go out the window with the renaming of a hundred American streets after Martin Luther King Jr. Shame on us for even needing to remind ourselves that Black lives matter. All lives matter, and our responsibility is to loudly voice that same proclamation and to do so in the name of the Church.

When we recognize that justice is being compromised, when we fail to acknowledge that any ethnic or socially disenfranchised peoples are being ignored and abused, it is our opportunity to actively promulgate change and move forward, seeking reconciliation for all. What rights do we have? One of our greatest sins may just be making our individual rights the center of our lives. Repentance is required, forgiveness awaits, and a challenge for renewal invites reconciliation for all.

***

---

5. *Mississippi Burning.*

What Rights Do We Have?

The teachings of Jesus can be so personal. If we pray long enough, if we pray hard enough, we usually can find some instruction and guidance relative to the best ways to work through not just routine but complex questions and challenges. Our first inclination is to turn to Scripture to unveil valuable teachings concerning our rights and the more appropriate ways we can repair our spirits as we wrestle with broken relationships and shattered ideals. The central question when we feel we have been treated unjustly should be, how are we to react to the injustice, the unpleasant, unfair treatment we have experienced? What rights, if any, do I have?

The irony is that we seldom find exact passages that spell out personalized instruction. This is especially true when we cannot consciously bend the Scriptural application to a more pleasant and egocentric conclusion. We are content, usually with less than adequate prayer and study, to generalize, often drafting our own answers based on some scant Biblical study, but mostly trusting a collection of personal assumptions that cluster around what we have predetermined to be the best way to address daily problems and frustrations.

What I am suggesting is simple. When offended or unjustly treated, we only conveniently borrow the idea of what would Jesus do. We can creatively alter the question to disavow any suggestion that we are acting out of our own personal convictions. Most of us respond to perceived social injustice far too independently, out of our own instruction, not in surrender to God's counsel. We feel comfortable in defending our actions by some pious platitude, bracketed by the claim "I am only doing what Jesus would do."

It is so emotionally dramatic to sheepishly utter that as a Christian, we love everyone and we avoid, at any costs, making unsolicited judgement. We are guilty of the shallowness and trite solution we assign to the personal injuries or criticisms we experience. We know, in truth, that our answers, when enacted in this condescending way, ultimately only lead to more frustration and pain. Cavalier, cynical responses do nothing less than breed more pain and frustration.

Any awareness of this teaching is sustaining, but the problem is how and when are these Godly blessings ours to claim? On what planet can we expect to enjoy them? When will God level the playing field and levy the appropriate punishment to my offenders, muzzling anyone whose voice has any variation to my own? For certain, answers sometimes seem to run short of the immediate and insufficient in utility. Our impatience, even our confusion, is best satisfied when we hear, "But they who wait for the Lord shall renew their strength, they shall mount up with wings like eagles; they shall run and not be weary; they shall walk and not faint" (Isa 40:31).

***

A fundamental awareness allows us to assume, as humankind, that we do have some rights. Most act as if this is an unequivocal truth and any arguments are in error if they suggest our rights should be restrained or should be submissive, especially if we do not really respect or even like the person who offends us. When insulted or harmed or unfairly rebuked, we naturally feel that some level of retribution is appropriate. The idea of *take it like a man* makes little sense. After all, we reason that surely the Bible says "an eye for an eye . . ." (Lev 24:20).

The idea of assuming entitlement is more than a casual intervention when we evaluate how we will react when offended. We can get a little cranky when we are required to acquiesce to demands, even restrictions, placed on us by individuals, institutions, even inalterable circumstance. We, with frustration, cry out, "Don't I have some 'rights' in the matter?" Do we not have rights when someone has insulted our intelligence or someone has blatantly misrepresented what we said or what we did; in fact, someone may have distorted our own personhood with inuendo or disdain. Maybe both.

Is there no recourse when someone else has taken credit for our hard work? After all, we invested the time and effort to ensure the product of our labor was a flawless demonstration of genuine accomplishment. We have invested the energy. We have tackled the limitless obstacles along the sordid and treacherous road to accomplishment. We have not just labored for the completion of the project, but also have desired perfection and full utility, but someone else is in a better position to gain all approval. It does not seem fair. Is there any recourse for us?

Must we resign in silence as we observe others whose approach to success is saturated with deceit, even tyranny? The harsh reality seems to allow that those who bully end up with reward while those bullied cower in shame and despair, left to wonder if they have any value at all. Far too many in the work force are recognized for their accomplishments while the persons doing the hardest work, laboring the longest of hours, and displaying the most visible stains of perspiration are relegated to sit quietly in the corner, their only reward to be passingly identified as part of the team.

I hate to be ignored. I grapple incisively with the temptation to cry out, "What's wrong with you people? Can't you see error in their thinking? I can't believe that you have bought into . . . ."

I am not proud of my disproportionate and frequently inappropriate feelings of frustration, not proud of unhinged, eruptive anger. Before my sentencing in the slammer, I am compelled to argue the point of reference from which I speak. My words can be ugly and hurtful, for sure, but occasionally I have remembered that Jesus raised a voice of condemnation to those who promoted injustice and burdensome harshness on the innocent. It is imperative that we prayerfully consider when and how righteous indignation is to find a proper place in our voices of protest. Often, what I am doing is justifying my own position, not by a sound argument but by some misguided attempt to disparage the person with whom I have disagreement. We, with some frequency, want desperately to release our muted judgmental thoughts, even utter profane words against the persons who lie, especially by way of gossip or innuendos. I want to just grab them and shake them and say, "What's wrong with you?" For certain, the poison tongue can inflict the greatest of pain on the most innocent of victims. It is difficult for the most spirit-filled among us to turn a cheek to those who so blatantly spread rumors and promote deceptive and misguided argument.

Most of the actions to which I have referred are, by nature, foolish. None of these thoughts, no single action against wrong, should be undertaken apart from the scrutiny of Scripture and should be released only through the fervency of conversation with the Heavenly Father. Reactionary responses must first and foremost be bridled. Motive must be honestly considered. Any action taken or words spoken must be carefully calibrated, and then, more than anything, emotions, especially those of anger and retaliation, must be checked. This reasoning, to me, makes Godly sense.

Jesus had much to say about retaliation, even revenge. He brought Old Testament law onto a level playing field. He did not just make it have consequence when broken but extended it to include infractions committed in everyday living. He took it from the temple to the street, from the mind of a nation to the heart of all people. Rules are made not only to prevent crime but to influence just living. It is better, by far, to start with the assumption that legal authorities are best identified as crime preventors, not just as law enforcers.

Jesus insisted that law was made for man and not man for the law. I am not quite sure what all that means. I think I do know what it does not mean. His comments, for certain, did not mean that we have no obligation to obey a law because it makes no sense to us or because, at one moment in time, we, by our obedience to the law, believe in its infallibility. Laws are written to be observed, and until they are adjudged by vote of the public to be amended or abolished, they must be observed. Jesus would not argue the point. What I do understand about the teaching of Jesus is that what He said makes sense. He seemed to constantly be expanding the meaning of not just life in general, but the variety of steps one takes toward authentic meaning and purpose—life as God intended it to be lived.

Regarding the Old Testament eye for an eye assumption, Jesus in no way attempted to weaken its value and importance to us. He took law to a new and fresher height. In Matthew 5:38–42, three stories are used to better illustrate the position Jesus took on retaliation. These are familiar stories. If you have been students of the scriptures for a while, no doubt you have been enlightened by the more poignant lesson each story reveals. There is a deeper teaching. If overlooked, confusion can set in, and we are left wondering if we have any option to fight back when abused or offended by someone. Let us take a look, for it is in these stories that Jesus expands and, in some ways, redefines the Old Testament law of retaliation.

Story 1: "You have heard that it was said, an eye for an eye and a tooth for a tooth. But I say to you, do not resist the one who is evil. But if anyone slaps you on the right check, turn to him the other also" (Matt 5:38, 39).

Story 2: "And if anyone would sue you and take your tunic, let him have your cloak as well" (Matt 5:40).

Story 3: "If anyone forces you to go with him one mile, go with him two miles" (Matt 5:41).

"My, my," as my three-year-old granddaughter recently spouted, "What we have here?" What we have are three very similar stories. All are entrenched in the same historic settings. In Palestine, Rome ruled the day. The Jews were under Roman authority, and Israel was subject to the burdens and hardships that were regularly being imposed on them. What Rome said was law, and the Jewish world was their subject.

Jesus told a few stories, all of which have much to do with the limited rights from which the Jewish world suffered. Retaliation was not the singular issue in the stories; certain customs, even restrictions, allowed by Roman law must be considered. All three stories address two fundamental realities, and all three describe a burdensome abuse of each character's human rights.

What Rights Do We Have?

Historians argue that the cheek slap in the first story was one of insult and was not only forbidden by Jewish practice but was also unlawful by Roman standards and could justify some legal recourse. This observation begs some additional word. Again, historians propose that, based on the fact that most people were right-handed, a slap on the right cheek would suggest that the action came by way of the back of the hand, a clear indication that he who initiated the action was guilty of a crime and could be prosecuted, that the subject of abuse could find some level of retribution.

Story two and story three also support the same latitude regarding retribution. Roman law allowed that a person engaged in a lawsuit could, if awarded favor, require the person to surrender his inner garment as partial payment. It was, however, illegal to demand he give up his outer coat. The cloak was necessary for survival in the frigid night air, and each person had a right to protect himself from nature's fury. Likewise, Israelites could be required, under certain conditions, to carry a Roman soldier's gear for up to a mile, but no further. The armor was extremely heavy. To assume support beyond the first mile was considered an abuse of rights and a display of unfair treatment. Legend has it that a popular phrase was often voiced: the first mile is Caesar's; the second belongs to God.[6] What we have in all three of our stories is evidentiary proof that Jewish citizens did have some rights and that an invitation to exercise those rights was protected by law.

***

The second point of the stories now comes into focus. Jesus seems to be suggesting that the true mark of discipleship is to be found, not just in obedience to the law, but in a willingness to go beyond one's rights to clearly display a level of character that is not only willing to forfeit one's rights but also willing to go far beyond. Given these historic details, does it not seem strange that Jesus would dare suggest that his followers do more than was expected of them? What he proceeds to tell them is that the focus of the believer is, first and foremost, on God, and second, it cannot, for authentic worship of him, be singularly on our own rights. It is that simple.

The first and unequivocal call on the believer is do no wrong. It starts with repentance and is validated by a commitment to responsible living. Next, and it is at this juncture that our three stories reveal ultimate truth, we are to operate in moral and ethical obedience with God's plan for his

---

6. When I used this quote in the original sermon, I did not cite its source.

creation, to reflect, in all things his nature. Last, and it is at this pivotal place that separation from an abandonment of the faith will most likely occur, we are to go the extra mile, do the unexpected, and act beyond the scope of our personal convenience.

To quench the thirst for retaliation and revenge is challenging. We feel justified, especially when the gravity of the injustice imposed on us is sharp and penetrating. We reason some response to hurt or insult inflicted from others cannot be overlooked. As believers, we try hard to ignore injurious and critical words from others, yet we may too often tell others the despicable way someone has insulted us and gone behind our backs to stymie our wellbeing or to cripple our enthusiasm. Jesus spoke of other solutions, but it goes against our grain to admit full credence to turning the other cheek.

No good pleasure ever comes from retaliation. Reactionary anger breeds greater conflict. It never results in getting even, but ensures, when pride has siphoned away all reasoning, that we are always the loser. In no way am I suggesting that modest defenses are forbidden—often words of explanation make more sense than bursts of rejection and denial. Going the extra mile can serve to repair damage done to our ego. The idea of "I will show him" is a one-way street. There is never a winner when our first course of action is to fight fire with fire. No one wins.

I suspect that most of us have been victims of the peril of bitterness. It is cancerous and appears to provide an exemption from necessary understanding as it argues for reactions that are exempt from extending forgiveness. We would rather not include forgiveness, openness, and understanding in our lists of options. Peace is usually a product of reconciliation, and if we are not willing to consider forgiveness, we easily become enslaved to our own methods of preservation—pouting, belligerence, contentiousness, militance, and overt sensationalism as we raise our nostrils so high that we best be praying for a dry summer.

The well-known twentieth century reformer Roland Bainton writes, "If in order to defeat the beast, one has to become a beast, has not bestiality won? I would say that one of the most subtle traps that evil sets for us is goading us into imitating the very thing we deplore in the name of righteous indignation."[7] Revenge is poisonous. Strife breeding strife is an endless cycle. One of my professors in seminary brought home an amazing, maybe often overlooked truth when he poignantly observed, "If you harbor hate for him who offends you, he has you right where he wants you. You

---

7. Bainton, *Here I Stand*.

are now under his control and your genuine rights have been forfeited."[8] Service to God seems often to operate with an escape plan, a jumping off point where allegiance to righteous living and loyalty to moral behavior can be abandoned successfully. We reason that it is not our place, the problem is not ours to solve, any involvement or responsible engagement is beyond our paygrade. For most, this excuse seems to have merit.

When we prayerfully choose to harness or even eliminate the many appeals to take action, we should not feel guilty. There are many good and worthy social, even political, challenges for which we should pray for resolution, but for which no further action on our part is necessary. However, the mission of the church cannot be compromised at the risk of distorting our purpose, at the risk of losing the values by which God called us. Jesus made it clear that government and the church have distinctive roles when he said, "Render to Caesar the things that are his and render to God the things that belong to Him" (Mark 12:17). Of course, constant prayer and constant service to each must be given.

Now that I have allowed the use of one or two get out of jail free cards, I feel I am in a better position to discuss the extent to which we *are* to take seriously the teachings of Jesus as exposed in our three stories. Buckle up. The ride may be a little bumpy. Hang on and rest assured that I include myself if any exposures to failure are uncovered. The ideas of going the extra mile, turning the other cheek, removing the shield on our insulated personhoods is serious business. It defines a shadowy world of faith we seldom explore, a terrain too remote and unfamiliar.

We are content to claim our rights but go no further. The three stories we have just casually examined must now, by necessity, be filed under the *duh* topic. They have lost any thunder they may have had in ancient times when economic and emotional survival were much less of a concern. The dog-eat-dog mentality is here to stay. The levels of humility to which all three of them refer is outdated; they have been lost in a world of the complicated and disheveled. They are, for the ambitious world of commerce, impractical; even the point they make is unnecessary for survival.

We carefully speculate that if we let down our guard and go beyond the expected, beyond our duty, people and a hundred good causes will take advantage of us. We argue that our way of thinking is realistic; it makes far more sense than some irrational crusade to right all the wrong in the world.

---

8. Harold Songer, Professor of New Testament Interpretation at Southern Baptist Theological Seminary, Louisville, KY, 1962–92.

Going any farther than a mile, turning the other cheek, extending charity beyond the flick of a coin would be debilitating if not foolish. Let someone whose time is less valuable than mine, whose skillset is more adequate, who has more knowledge take on the project, stand in the gap. If we go out of our way to work with the homeless or the hopeless, we risk too much and subject ourselves to not only personal danger, but also to irreparable emotional damage, a pain we think we should avoid at all costs.

I certainly am not sure that I personally can find the spiritual resolve to legitimize turning the other cheek or giving in or giving up my most precious possessions, especially if it is not necessary, if doing so may fail to make any difference. If we, in truth, expend the necessary spiritual and emotional energy, I suspect we can find a hundred different ways to actualize our commitment to Jesus—ways to extend our faith beyond the expected to the sacrificial. Genuine sacrifice and personal vulnerability may not always be a necessity, but it is the standard to which our Lord points us.

For more expanded insight, let us look at the reactionary climate following the death of George Floyd. Can we learn from the event and see if anything insightful surfaces, if any message or instruction awaits a deeper probe? For certain, nearly everyone on the planet has been subjected to some level of modified thinking concerning the event. Media coverage alone has ensured that our moral, emotional, even our spiritual needles have inched either to the right or to the left. Who could avoid some stirring of the conscience, some suspension of the norm with confusion lingering nearby? We have all been shaken and, most of all, challenged to reexamine what we really believe, to experience an honest probing of the inner spirit.

I have already allowed that guilt is not to be experienced if we determine that the protest march is not for us. On the other hand, if we choose to avoid a more divinely inspired analysis of injustice, it may suggest our indifference is showing and our call to righteous living is far too minimized. Too often, at the risk of offending, I have closed the door and chosen to avoid getting involved or have lacked the courage to make known my concerns to friends, to other churchmen. Jesus never presumed that embracing our rights was the station where we can sneak off the salvation train and hustle away to be lost in the crowd. Christianity is an active and ongoing process. It has never been assumed that doing the ordinary, doing only what we can get away with, is the place at which comfort is to be our reward. To rely on that kind of thinking is a bit calloused when the gravity and universalism of the death of George Floyd is in clear sight and cannot be ignored.

What Rights Do We Have?

Open and honest dialogue is usually accompanied by some strategies for repair and forward momentum. Police reform, new and more logical legislation, social and economic betterment for all must not be delayed, cannot be shoved under the carpet. It has been there far too long. It has been skillfully hidden under the misguided assumption that we have arrived. Editorially speaking, we will not arrive until the Lord returns, but to rest on that affirmation is to link arms with the foolish virgins who were content with their half-full urns of oil (Matt 25:1–13).

We cannot ignore the voices being broadcast. We need to confess our own personal inadequacies, repent, and trust our Lord for divine instruction. Maybe it is time we take a stand and open ourselves in a renewed commitment to justice and understanding. Any stand we take, any voice we raise, may be risky; it may even, as I have experienced, weaken if not damage a relationship with a lifelong friend. The *here I stand* mentality must not, at every given moment, be hamstrung by our stubborn wills. Now may be the time for it to be unleashed and lovingly, gently, and unashamedly spoken.

Several important observations have personally grabbed me. Number one, as I have attempted to humbly confess elsewhere in this document, though childhood innocence can soften the guilt, I grew up with a genuine prejudice toward African Americans. I was aware of it. I just did not understand, until recently, that it has remained with me, albeit in veiled and unspoken ways, until this day. The real tragedy is that it has never quite gone away, for me or for society. Enormous strides have been made and continue to be made now. However, the sin that we most need to confess is that the progress and the attitudinal changes we profess have been allowed to disintegrate beneath the surface of our indifference and our selfish, lustful passions. Our objectives have been far too focused on building, through economic and technological progress, a great America. There is nothing wrong with progress, that is, unless its only value and ultimate end is selfish and overly personalized. The moral fabric of each step taken toward fairness and equality must be examined ultimately through the lens of Judeo-Christian thinking.

Bigotry and selfishness have flourished while the value and dignity of every person, regardless of color, has been compartmentalized or even ignored. It is obvious that the profiling of Black Americans and other ethnic groups is still a cancer with which God is not happy, nor should we be. I personally was not ever tempted to join a protest march. It was not just because of the looting and property destruction that accompanied the protest marchers. We should be smart enough to recognize that the real and compassionate voices for change abhor these untoward actions. In fact, these misguided and illegal activities dampen the arguments for change and fairness.

The majority of demonstrators hoped to make the statement that Black lives matter and that all lives matter. Their actions were to remind us that now may be the time for some much-needed adjustments to not only the judicial system but to the mindset of those chosen to administer the rights drafted for the protection and security of each citizen. Because we have, in the past, successfully raised voices for change, a renewed commitment and sustainable hope has been ignited. It has resurfaced more vividly, but not without pain, the fear of being offensive, and the rejection of many.

Renewed energy for good is never without some misguided enthusiasm. Actions, whether good or not so good, must, by necessity, be identified and adjudicated. Hopefully, good and much improved days are ahead. The major fear I have is that the necessary voices for change have been so shrouded by partisan politicizing that the energy for any forward momentum will lose much of its vitality. Only time will determine the accuracy to my amateur forecast. I think Jesus would have a voice in this matter. I think, for sure, He would remind us that attention must be given to the problems of systemic unfairness and prejudice. It is still very present in this country; in fact, it is still present in the world. He would remind us that doing only what is expected of us falls short of genuine discipleship. He would say that we are not to do just enough to sustain normalcy, but to embrace a fresh and powerful voice in support of fairness and equality for all.

His admonition would start with a call for repentance. He would remind us that ignoring the realities and sins of forgetfulness and ignorance cannot go unnoticed, cannot go unchanged. We need to be reminded that we are not to go just a mile; we need to invest adequate time and effort and resources to complete the journey. A "more than is required" effort is the surest path to recovery and wholeness. Maybe some from the church should join the peaceful protests. The world needs to know where we stand. Maybe some should work harder for legislative change or greater investments in better education and living environments for those who are forced to live in less than adequate housing. Maybe others should seize an opportunity for public voice on a platform of reform and fairness. The list really can be expanded exponentially. Each person needs some involvement in the drafting of its content. Prayer is powerful, but participation must always be the higher option.

Now for a few concluding thoughts. The idea of doing the unexpected can nudge at our hearts. Just to write of it has made me squirm a little in my seat. We really do not need to feel major guilt for not being more visible in our positions on social and political issues. In many instances, we are not adequately trained or qualified for accurate and fair judgements. However, I think it is of value that we daily repent of our misguided reasoning and of our indifferences to issues impacting the value and dignity of man. The *here I stand* message still has an important place in the church. Most of us in the church, I suspect, have experienced the joy and the exhilaration of expending, of doing less than glamorous deeds, of making above average effort. My wife and I can provide endless stories of personal victories experienced in the sacrifice of self when we worked with a homeless ministry. We would not trade most of those times for anything. Our efforts are only a microcosm of the standards of discipleship established by Jesus.

The story of Ruth cries for an honored place to illustrate the point. Who could forget the drama? In desperation, Elimelech, his wife Naomi, and their two sons, Mahlon and Chilion, left their famine-plagued home in Bethlehem of Judah and settled into a strange land where they discovered sustenance and security. To feel comfortable and safe is a fundamental right for which we all aspire. Their arrival in the land of Moab was smooth and secure. Both sons married. Suddenly, out of nowhere, as life far too often does, the family was dealt harsh reality. Not only did Elimelech die; both sons also died. As good fortune has it, Naomi was graciously and lovingly cared for by her two daughters-in-law, Orpah and Ruth.

When living conditions dramatically improved in Judah, Naomi was compelled to return to her homeland. Although Orpah and Ruth were not obligated to leave the familiarity and comfort of home, they both elected to do the right thing and go with Naomi. We see at a critical juncture in the story exposure to the moment of truth for Orpah and Ruth. Both had done their duty. Both Orpah and Ruth had extended compassion beyond expectancy. But now, their extra mile challenge faced them. They both elected to travel, with Ruth, to the place of her God where life really began for her. Naomi, recognizing the extent of sacrifice both women were willing to make, offered them a gracious path of honored retreat. She encouraged them to give a second thought to their loving act of loyalty.

Orpah reconsidered her decision and accepted Naomi's offer. Ruth, however, was resolute. She had determined that her loyalty to Naomi might not bring to her personally the comfort and security of home, but it would validate her commitment and her willingness to extend to her mother-in-law the same love she had for her husband. The fear of the unfamiliar was replaced with the true emotion of sacrifice and vulnerability. From her decision, those familiar and powerful words resonate as testimony to Ruth's willingness to step into the unknown: "Do not urge me to leave you or to return from following you. For where you go, I will go, and where you lodge, I will lodge. Your people shall be my people and your God my God. Where you die, I will die, and there will I be buried. May the Lord do so to me and more also if anything but death parts me from you" (Ruth 1:16, 17).

The truth is that Jesus went more than the extra mile. For him, total obedience was death. Apart from the Holy Bible, the one book that perhaps has influenced me most is *Through Gates of Splendor* by Elisabeth Elliot. Many will remember the story of the five missionary men who died violently at the hand of the Auca Indians, in Ecuador, on the northwest coast of South America. I was so moved by the fact that these were educated men with families and children who seemingly had every opportunity to live the American dream. Instead, they chose servanthood, a calling that ultimately led to the tragic death of all five. Jim Elliot's words, uttered just before the fatal flight into the jungles of the Auca Indians, tells the story: "Well, if that's the way God wants it to be," he said in response to his wife's reasoning that they both knew what it might mean if he went into the jungle, "I am ready to die for the salvation of the Aucas."[9] While a student in college Elliot had written, "He is no fool who gives what he cannot keep, to gain what he cannot lose."[10]

Working with the homeless and the sacrificial witness of the five missionaries have a strange and silent commonality—both were done in obedience to God's call. Neither invited indifference. Both promised real victory. Both were validated by the resurrection of Jesus. Rewards for our labors are now, at best, partial, not yet fully given. One of the shortest sermons every preached was by an old black pastor who stood before his congregation and offered, with simple but profound meaning, "Friday is happenin', but

---

9. Elliot, *Through Gates of Splendor*, 58.
10. Elliot, *Through Gates of Splendor*, 58.

Sunday is a comin.'"[11] He then sat down. To go the extra mile, to turn the other cheek, to help carry the burden of a brother is reward unspeakable.

---

11. Lockridge, *It's Friday, But Sunday's Comin'*.

Chapter 25

Our Search for God

Pray then like this:
Our Father in heaven,
Hallowed be your name.
Your kingdom come,
your will be done,
on earth as it is in heaven.
Give us this day our daily bread,
and forgive us our debts,
as we also have forgiven our debtors.
And lead us not into temptation,
but deliver us from evil (Matt 6:9–13).

For you did not receive the spirit of slavery to fall back into fear, but you have received the Spirit of adoption as sons, by whom we cry, "Abba! Father! The Spirit himself bears witness with our spirit that we are children of God, and if children, then heirs—heirs of God and fellow heirs with Christ, provided we suffer with him in order that we may also be glorified with him (Rom 8:15–17).

TOM WOLFE, AMERICAN AUTHOR and journalist, makes a profoundly penetrating statement reflective of a fundamental teaching concerning the nature of God. He eloquently offers, "The deepest search of life, it seems to me, the thing that in one way or another is central to all living, is man's search for a Father; not merely the father of his flesh, nor merely the father of his lost youth but the image of a strength and wisdom eternal to his need and superior to his hunger; one to which the belief and power of his own life could be united."[1]

Something deep inside of us cries out for a reality that is, at once, within us and yet beyond us. We passionately desire relating to a divine *someone* who is the magnification of the love and tenderness of one or both parents. Our search for God is a yearning for a relationship of intimacy. I understand that the abandonment of a father or a mother, even the lack of knowing either, may leave scars too deep, too calloused to even admit such an assumption, but it does for most of us seem to be true.

In 1967, Remington Rand manufactured a typewriter with a keyboard that included a controversial punctuation mark identified as an *interrobang*.[2] Literary geniuses of the day had recognized that several words and expressions possessed the dual interpretation of both the interrogative and the exclamatory. As an example, expressions like *you call that a book, you're dying, what are those* are statements that could invite exclamation or question mark. Of course, when spoken, inflection would help distinguish the meaning, but when written, the options for exact meaning might be more challenging. History records, as the solution, the design of an obtuse punctuation mark. The interrobang, in most instances, is depicted by a question mark with an exclamation symbol superimposed on it. Production of the special typewriter, with its answer to the confusion, was soon abandoned because of rapidly diminishing sales and crumbling popularity. The distinction between exclamatory and interrogative was again left to context, and the interrobang is, today, all but forgotten.

In a sense, the prayer Jesus taught his disciples to pray does possess an *interrobang* moment where two distinctive characteristics of God find expression as one. The Lord's prayer records the unique and profound way by which God is to be defined as both the loving Abba Father and the God of heaven, representing the permanency and meaning of all creation. He truly is the *I am, that I am*. To understand and to know him through this exposure is, for most of humankind, the beginning of genuine faith.

---

1. The source for this quote has long ago been lost but the internet is replete with quotes that both stimulate thought and evoke humor.

2. Houston, *The Interrobang*.

Gift Revisited

***

The phrase "our father who is in heaven" brings immediate and recognizable awareness, an emotion that transcends the boundaries of curiosity, an aspiration that aligns with our hunger for acceptance and forgiveness. To discover a probability that there is some alternate guardianship beyond this veil of human mystery, a source for strength and sustainability, not only awakens in humankind a thirst to know God but reminds us that there is the possibility of a repair for the brokenness that has resulted from the realities of sin.

The Lord's model prayer opens with immutable promise that captures, in only a few words, the possibility that ensures transformation of the human spirit. The Lord's passionate words portend salvation for the disenfranchised spirit as well as hope for those whose lives and dreams are mournfully deplete of security and for those left wanting in self-respect. Scripture is replete with the adoption motif. Its importance is unquestionable. The adoption of Israel is seen from the call of Abram to the protective preservation of a nation. The story is graphically depicted in the Exodus narrative. God's redemptive adoption is again announced at Sinai and is marked by the covenant relationship. All seems to suggest that the *our Father* relationship has, from the beginning, been a divine possibility, an act of divine providence.

One tender and extraordinary point of reasoning is used by adoptive parents to explain to the child their decision for adoption. We are emotionally moved to hear the logic that adoptive children were *chosen* based on real-time experiences. The element of choice, in so many ways, validates the extraordinary love shared in the adoptive parent/child relationship. *We chose you to be part of our family* is an acknowledgement that is not always so true, not easily uttered, in every parent of birth circumstance.

It is not to deny that birth parents do not love their child in advance of the actual birth, but it is to say that adoptive parents have the advantage of observable information that contributes to and further defines their choice. Even though the logic may still not completely reduce all questioning related to self-worth, the adopted child can never deny the degree to which his adoptive parents have gone to demonstrate their love and their desire to, with the child, celebrate family.

God's unique relationship with humankind is vividly demonstrated in the garden of creation. The immutable and impassioned phrase, *God walked with them,* tells the story in profound and irrevocable truth. It is undeniable evidence of the Father/child connection between the created and the Creator. Fellowship with the Father is not only a possibility but is also undeniable. The intimacy of God's conversation with man, when understood and accepted, represents his willingness to relate to his creation, but more importantly, it is a divine confirmation of God's eternal and ultimate design: that not any should perish but that all would find relationship, recognizing and embracing connection with the *our Father* about whom Jesus so passionately spoke.

Fatherly and creative dialogue suggests the possibility of genuine knowledge and understanding. In a sense, the choice Adam and Eve made to disrupt the conversation with God led to their sin. A gulf between the Creator and the created is in stark contrast to God's original design. Jesus brought the *good news* back into focus. He is the way and the truth (John 14:6).

***

Joachim Jeremias, a German Lutheran theologian and scholar, captured the essence of the God to whom Tom Wolfe, quoted earlier, alludes. In his powerful little book entitled *The Lord's Prayer*, Jeremias carefully explores the way in which mankind grapples to understand the nature of God.[3] He argues that the opening stanza of the model prayer poignantly identifies the two-dimensional axis on which man's understanding of God is balanced.

He begins his analysis with the familiar understanding of the phrase, *Abba Father*. As any good student of language will remember, Jesus distinctively identifies the Heavenly Father in this warm and personalized manner. It is the loving and tender expression that enables the listener to understand that we can be connected spiritually to one who is like our daddy. His acceptance of us is a commodity of grace. For man, the *Abba Father* expression points singularly to the possibility of a unique relationship with the creator God. Even the most insensitive among us recognizes the need for a God who offers love and acceptance. However, to seriously search for His nearness with any openness and sincerity is all but forgotten by the consuming attitude that argues, "I can make it on my own."

---

3. Jeremias, *Lord's Prayer*.

Sadly, self-aggrandizement wins out in the end. Many are resistant to believing in a god that will chain them to a boring and mundane existence. They feel that pleasure and joy will vanish from their grip and a transformative lifestyle will relegate them to some extended punishment for past ineptitude. I know from personal experience that this attitude enslaved me as a child in rural West Virginia. This attitude and distorted way of thinking were prevalent in a world of rugged individualism, one where passion for success was defined by control and power. This was a world and a time in history when achievement and success were measured more by who up the holler was first to own the seventeen inch, black and white Bendix television than it was by who was the first to extend compassion and forgiveness beyond their insulated worlds of self-preservation.

The idea of Black Lives Matter was so far out of reach that not one person gave any second thought to the existence of something called systemic racism. The sad truth was that liberation from the daily slavery of the "colored" was only an embryonic thought in the minds of a relative few. On a few visits back to West Virginia, I became aware that many of the young men with whom I grew up had, years after I moved away, come to faith in Christ. These were acquaintances, most of whom were a little older than me. Some were even distant relatives. When I knew them, a few were already married but were still holding onto their macho man persona.

When I learned of their spiritual transformation, my first reaction was to celebrate the changes in these men, recalling as I did the anguish through which their families had gone fearing that their child would end up an alcoholic or in prison. I admit that I found these feel-good stories quite compelling. These men were those who were hesitant to have anything to do with church, even though families had been praying ceaselessly for their salvation.

Now, why the change? I am sure the reasons are abundant, but I suspect many grew up with the distorted view of God to which I earlier referred. They could not accept that God loved them. Deep inside, they struggled to even love themselves. Their value systems were fueled by tangible, measurable achievement, most of which had found only momentary worth for them in the glory days of their youth. To be captain of the high school football team and to end up married to the homecoming queen just was not enough.

When faced in young adulthood with the immenseness and challenges of the adult world, their attitude toward faith had experienced a metamorphosis. They had, at last, come to understand that God loved them in an *Our Father* kind of way. Perhaps they had finally learned that the God about whom they had been taught not only loved them but was also a God who claimed all authority and power over their lives. They had for a time ignored this reality by hit-or-miss living. Finally, they had come to a place where faith took on clearer meaning. They learned that faith in Christ was not singularly the acceptance of God as daddy nor was he some disciplinary tyrant who wanted to wreak havoc on their joy. The *otherness of God* had been included in their thinking. This discovery is the necessary and accepted evidence of a genuine transformational faith.

If God is no more than our daddy, then we are reducing, not expanding, our faith in a creator whose cosmic power, whose better wisdom is no more than a popular hero in some glossy comic book. My old acquaintances in West Virginia had come to understand that this line of reasoning was a one-way relationship: He saves us from a fitful tragedy while we applaud him with no evidence that something transformative has taken place in our lives. This muffled understanding defines a God who ingratiates himself by issuing clemency as he unveils to us: "I'm okay, you're okay." We find good pleasure in the casualness of this one-way relationship while any acceptance of his lordship over our lives is muted and ineffective. Here we have a classic example of man wanting to control God and not an acknowledgement that he is the Lord of creation over all things.

There is danger if we allow light to shine too squarely, even allowing it to reveal singular focus on the *Abba Father* chapter of our faith walk. Any heavy concentration on God in this way can weaken our resolve and commitment to responsible living. The danger is simple. Seeing God only as our buddy is an emotional invitation to exclude *his otherness*. Our union with the God of heaven becomes, then, a one-sided relationship.

My thinking on this subject is often validated by the "health and wealth voices" who teach that blessings and rewards are at the disposal of any child of God who will only trust and claim the bounty so abundantly cheap. In my judgment, this is an egregious misuse of one's faith in Christ. This compulsory act by some marginalizing church leaders produces great numbers in their congregations but does little to acknowledge the invitation of Christ, who bid his followers *to come and die*. Please don't get me wrong. I have enjoyed fellowship with brothers whose focus was on the "just trust and you will receive" way of thinking. My major concern, however, has always been the absence of any evidence of sustainability promised from a heavy dose of this kind of religion. It can bring disappointment and even, for many, an ultimate abandonment of faith.

During my days in the pulpit, I found it difficult to support the "rapture of the church" theory popularized in the early 1970s by Hal Lindsey. To me, the teaching was inconsistent regarding the path of discipleship to which Jesus pointed.[4] My struggle is that the teaching of Lindsey, and many others, on the rapture of the church suggests that it is to take place during the great tribulation. This teaching seems to focus exclusively on the Abba Father way of knowing God. Lindsey's book, *The Late Great Planet Earth*, successfully lit a prophetic match under an exegesis of Revelation 4:1b.[5] In my judgement, the flame dramatically distorted evidence of the final victory for the church; instead it lit a celebration sparkler with the misguided reference to *come up hither*, the statement consistently used to support the theory that the church will not go through the time of great tribulation.

The Revelator clearly did not intend to say that the Church was to be raptured and dragged away from the period of tribulation—thus the misguided focus on the *come up hither* reference. We should remember, at all costs, that the rain falls on the just and the unjust (Eccl 5:15, 18–20; Matt 5:45}. Nowhere in Scripture do I find the teaching that believers are exempt now or in the future from the perils and inconsistencies of life. This is not to argue that God does not choose to intervene in the affairs of humankind, but it is meant to acknowledge that the divine intervention is not based on the high levels of obedience we daily exercise. I seriously doubt that we can ever know the reasons behind God's compassionate interventions. They are of his choosing, not ours.

The Scofield Reference Bible promoted this theory from its first publishing in 1917,[6] and such thinking has raised an ugly head on many occasions ever sense. Bible scholars can chase this rabbit all the way back to J. N. Darby in England.[7] Revelation 4:1b is clearly a visionary reference from which an eschatological perspective can be noted, and it does provide assurance that the ultimate victory of good over evil cannot be denied. The

---

4. Lindsay, *Late Great Planet Earth*.

5. "After this I looked, and behold, a door was opened in Heaven and the first voice I heard was, as if it were as a trumpet talking with me: which said, 'come up Hither, and I will show you things which must be hereafter.'"

6. Scofield, *The Scofield Reference Bible*.

7. John Nelson Darby (1800–1829), an Anglo-Irish Bible teacher, was one of the influential figures among the original Plymouth Brethren and the founder of the Exclusive Brethren. He is considered to be the father of modern Dispensationalism and Futurism.

going out to meet him in the air is just that; it is a greeting of the victorious King. It does not portend an escape from tribulation, but a celebration of God's victory over evil.

Nothing in Scripture seems to promise that a life lived in faith brings an abundance of fame and prosperity. For certain, God's abiding love and protection never leave us, but to assume that in the brokenness of creation, flashcards for successful living are readily distributed to those who will only believe is flawed, misguided thinking. The assumption that believers will be escorted to safety when that terrible day of fear and lostness arrives, be it seven years or seventy in length, smells of misguided and wishful thinking. In the context of Biblical history, it just does not make sense.

The unproportionate interplay between the *Abba Father* and the *who is in heaven* seems to have reduced God to a vending machine mentality. To selfishly assume that when overcome by desperation, we can march over to the machine, passionately pull the most attractive lever, and witness the immediate and appealing bundle of blessings gingerly falling into the reward tray defines, in my judgement, a faith that is one-dimensional, and more often than not, it quickly evolves into disappointment, if not tragedy.

***

To know that there is a God who loves and accepts us is the beginning of the faith journey, not the summation of a divine relationship. Genuine faith is discovering that we can only know God and his supremacy as it is defined from two points of reference. Until that is admitted, true knowledge of God is incomplete. The thirst to know a Heavenly Father is defined by acknowledging God as Abba Father. We must equally strive to know a Creator who is unlike the selfish and ugly side of us. He is a loving Father who never accepts as right the sinful elements of our personhood. Until we recognize that God hates sin, we can never truly embrace him as *daddy*.

I remember, as if it happened just a few days ago, having some deeper thoughts concerning the nature of God. For most, in some form or the other, this can be, or maybe should be, a daily activity. This day of reflection was, for me, different. Any attempt to find further explanation as to its origin is not necessary. Maybe the drudgery of the day or the fatigue of the drive home resulted in a level of contemplation more logically suited for some parallel universe. More than likely, I was disheveled, my thinking clouded by some desire to be profound. Who knows? I have spent a lot of my life daydreaming, looking for answers to questions I really do not know how to ask.

My thinking was being consumed by John 3:16, a verse so familiar that understanding for the verse never seemed to be in question. *For God so loved* . . . . What thought could be more profound? But yet, there was something in my heart that day that felt obscure, something that suggested not all the mystery in John 3:16 had, for me, been exposed. I thought about the fact that dogs love their owners. After all we feed and provide care for them. There is no demand from the animal that we respond, with some emotional commitment to their value system. Even if we forget or even if we fail to take the best care of them, they seem to still love us. They require no reaction, good or bad, to validate their love for us or our love for them. They want, at least some do, to play, to hunt, to bark. Even when mistreated, they seem to want to please. Their brief moments of cowering when anticipating discipline vanish quickly. Soon the tail vigorously wags again.

But John 3:16 seems, at least to me, to have some additional message. For sure, it clearly reminds that God loves me. However, it is the *whosoever believeth* that compels a closer look. Without question, we know that God loves all; each is precious in his sight. What John wanted me to know is that seeing God as Abba Father is only the first acknowledgement for a true relationship. Is Abba Father not also worthy of my action of belief? Does that act not equally mean an acknowledgement of our lostness, one that includes a commitment to a new lordship, a life lived in a covenant relationship? I think so. When I accept the love of my dog, it is assumed that I will take care of him. However, I still retain the choice to follow through with that action. When we authentically come to know God in his fulness, the choice has been made for us. Do we easily and joyfully live in that covenant relationship? No! But we are perpetually tied to that covenant, and any judgment for our failures absolved on a bleak hill known as Calvary.

Salvation is made possible through the redemptive work of Jesus. Even if we grew into our faith and cannot identify the moment of covenant, even if many in remote jungles or in the famished deserts of this world have never pronounced his name, even if the worship style of many sects and denominations seems to us remote, obscure, or inadequate to provide authenticity, someone else's faith is not subjected to our approval or disapproval. The Abba Father has, for all time and eternity, reserved for all peoples the right to either follow or reject Him.

Our Search for God

The view by which one attempts to envision God is, in fact, not a choice that yields attraction to one attribute over the other. It, by divine standards, is not an *either-or* but a *both-and* understanding at which man must arrive to authentically know God. If we succumb to a pick and choose approach, any effort to fully know him is void of authentic value. Jesus recognized that compartmentalizing the attributes of God dangerously resembled the pantheism of his days, the watering down of God's divine nature, and that leads to a misguided and faulty faith. Israel was emerging out of a world where constant battle had been waged against cultures whose worship found expression by allegiance to many gods. There seemed to be a compendium of gods for every need, resulting in an endless and confusing array of choices.

Paul encountered the absurdity of this theological hodge-podge when he stood on Mars Hill to preach his Jesus apologetic at the Areopagus (Acts 17:22–31). It appears that a multiplicity of gods was in evidence. Luke notes that the Athenians, to ensure that every conceivable other-worldly authority was recognized, had even erected an altar to an unknown god (Acts 17:23). Paul knew that the Christ, the Jesus of Nazareth, offered to all men, both Jew and Gentile, his love and acceptance. He was convinced that Jesus held the authority and power of heaven, as evidenced by his resurrection. Jesus instructed, "In this manner we pray." He quietly taught, in his model prayer, truth as it relates to the nature of God. Our Heavenly Father loves us, and our Heavenly Father rules a creation that was built with logic and balance and harmony and productivity. For one to live authentically within the framework of this system, both elements of God's nature must be observed.

***

Hopefully, my earlier observation confirms that an authentic search to know the God of creation includes the integration of two intimately related characteristics. Each holds a distinctive point of origin, but neither can be separated from the other. It must be accepted that the *Abba Father* and the *who art in heaven* realities are not two sides of a coin; they are minted in the sameness of truth. We cannot seek a God who is loving without including, in our search, a God who wants to deliver us from the blights of a fallen creation.

Can any value be enjoyed by professing a God who is the better image of ourselves? The *otherness* of God is the only real assurance of genuine hope. Much of the world is content to confess allegiance to a god whose

Gift Revisited

place in our faith is validated by our wishful thinking and by some *get out of jail free card*. They make an acknowledgement that invites only a shallow and precipitous cadence toward an unrealized allegiance. When the nature of God is defined by our hunger for a god who is best personified by manufactured superlatives that make him resemble some sort of superman, we are limiting the very essence of God. Genuine faith is born out of both the love and the otherness of God. Love forgives our sin when the confession of that sin is to the Creator who authored the standard by which that sin is adjudged.

To assume that faith in God is outside righteous and constructive living creates a faith void and empty. It fosters a belief system without any real awareness of the Godly standard by which we are intended to live. If this teaching is neglected, sin has found its place. This way of rationalization is an open invitation to lawlessness and greed, neither of which will find any level of meaningful influence in our lives. Humility, the hallmark of faith, vanishes from the grasp of those who forget that God not only loves and accepts them, but also calls each believer to Godly living.

As I write on the nature of God, news has arrived that another evangelical hero has bit the dust. The standards for authentic faith have once again suffered a painful blow by the lifestyle examples of Jerry Falwell Jr.[8] His recent acts of questionable behavior have provided yet one more reason for the sceptics to point an accusatory finger at the church. Our spirits can be distorted and confused as we journey through the maze of our broken world. We can find ourselves locked into a lifestyle of altered and compromised truth. When we appear to be seeking a voice from God, the sound seems distorted and weak. Society keeps redefining truth. People in whom we want to have trust fail us. Certainties and uncertainties merge in bewildering contradiction.

The dilemma of what to believe finds authentic value when our pursuit for knowledge and understanding is intimately tied to the *who art in heaven* way of understanding God. Truth does exist, despite those who distort it by faulty thinking and disenfranchising compromise. Absolutes do exist. Standards by which to identify Godliness are not precariously relegated to shadow and cannot be marginalized by casual reflections of what feels good, what I think of as a proper and acceptable conduct while I muddle along with my head lodged somewhere in the clouds. Reasonable thinking guarded by Biblical teachings can be recognized not by inebriated

---

8. Severns et al., "They All Got Careless."

misgivings or selfish inuendo. Only through an openness to the voice of the Holy Spirit of a loving God can the true standards of Godliness be perceived: "You shall know the truth and the truth will set you free" (John 8:32).

As I think about the nature of God and man's search to know him, I realize first that the subject is not one which I can easily wrap my arms around. I understand intellectually the assumptions at which Jeremias arrived. His insight has been very helpful. In fact, I think he was on the right path to understanding. His efforts to arrive at a place that illuminates the questions we must ask in our quest to know God provides an amazing roadmap by which the authentic journey to faith can be launched.

By way of conclusion, the duel understanding of God does not allow value to one characteristic over the other, but the merging together of both elements does produce ideals and patterns of knowledge that more exactly define the nature of God. It moves us from fundamental truth to more specific illustrative awareness. As we come to accept and understand the simplicity and exactness of Jesus' teaching, we discover more clearly, through experience and the exposure to truth, the nature of God. We can personally know him through both the heart and the head.

As a sometimes over-thinker, I want to take Jeremias' reasoning further by attempting not only to illustrate his teaching, but also to find a few personal applications to shed light on my own understanding. Perhaps it is accurate to call my add-ons ancillary attributes from which additional insight might be possible. Forgiveness of sin, for example, is best authenticated through God as both *Abba Father* and God *who is in heaven*. Without acknowledging both, the process is incomplete. Jesus, the Christ, was sinless. His journey into the desert to be tested of Satan gives evidence of his God nature. There the attraction of each temptation was an invitation to succumb to the thirst for fame and power, yet Christ denied each satanic gift he was offered. He did so because he loved us (Abba Father) and because he would, through his ministry, demonstrate his surrender to the plan and purpose of his heavenly Father, the Abba Father whose standards cannot be compromised. God's way is, in fact, absolute—"not my will but thine be done" (Mark 14:36, Luke 22:47).

For certain, man has misused and abused this teaching by distorting and manufacturing, for personal pleasure, his own definitions of what is right and acceptable behavior. The fogginess of the lens through which our actions are adjudged is to better sustain our egos. If we play around with and attempt to alter, in self-gratifying action, the moral and natural law to compensate for disappointment and failure, we might accelerate the appearance of an emotional disaster just waiting to happen. In our efforts to justify our *this is what I want, and this is what I will have* reasoning, disasters will inevitably overtake us.

Regardless of how hard we try, we will ultimately never emotionally survive on the singular assumption that God loves us. Faithfulness is defined by our allegiance and service to a God who transcends our humanness. He is a God who built into his creation a system of order. Through our adherence to this structure, productive and responsible living is to be actualized.

The experience concerning the nature of God's forgiveness is powerfully illustrated and consistently finds agreement in Jesus' encounter with the woman at the well. The story powerfully illustrates the immutable truth of fully accepting *God as Father* while acknowledging God as *He who is in heaven*. Both elements are present in this story. Forgiveness does not stand as a third element to better define God; it is a merging together of both characteristics and is descriptive of a God who loves us, a God who is fully aware of our sin nature, and a God who requires recompence for it. The *payment* answer for sin is possible only when the source of forgiveness is through one's personal acceptance of the work done at Calvary. It is only through our exposure to and confession of our lostness that freedom from sin is possible.

The news is good. Exposure to our sin and forgiveness of it brings not condemnation but joy and freedom from guilt and enables us to walk not in arrogance and pride but in hope and in the promise of life abundant. John 4:1–45 records Jesus' penetrating conversation with the woman at the well. She was clearly captive to her sin. Numerous sexual relations had rendered her an outcast. She had to stand in the shadows listening while others whispered the endless details of her sordid lifestyle. Clearly her spirit was incarcerated. She knew no freedom.

Along came Jesus, who knows the human soul. After all, he had come to set the captive free. He did not provide a freedom that affords more reckless living and loyalty to an unbridled will, but one that brings new value and a new freedom. He was pointing her not to the repair of an outworn imperialism but to a new freedom, a freedom that would provide her a release from all that besets the human spirit. The thirst to know a Creator of that immense magnitude and power invites her repeated exclamation, "I met a man, come see . . ." (John 4:29).

In study of the poignant Holy Scripture, we discover that John 4 is reminding us that when forgiven, we find a new release and a new freedom. The natural result, or at least it should be, is that now we are compelled to tell others about the man, Jesus. His love and our exposure to sin is a consummate definition of a God who is both *Abba Father* and *who is in heaven*. The Samaritan woman had ended her search for ultimate meaning. Evidence is clearly revealed; the joy, the freedom could not be contained. In verse 25 the woman reasons regarding the promised Messiah, "I know that when he comes, he will tell us all things." In verse 29 she reports to the townspeople, "Come see a man who told me all that I ever did." In verse 39, the townspeople (both men and women) are enthralled by her words as she repeats, "He told me all that I ever did."

The point here is simple. As humankind we naturally fear exposure to our sin. Many times, we work extremely hard to keep it hidden. That protective reasoning deters us from accepting God's love, but it also compels us to shield ourselves from admittance of the influence of the sins to which we are held captive. When we *meet a Man* who is fully God and fully aware of our sin, but applies forgiveness to that shameful reality, it can and should be the most liberating experience imaginable. We can joyfully, without fear of rejection, grounded in a new resolve to righteous living, exclaim, "Come meet a man."

We fear exposure to our sins. We may cloud them over, cross them off by thinking, "I didn't realize the harmful nature of . . . , it's not that big of a deal, I can stop at any time, I can't let anyone find out." The list goes on and on, but, as our friend at the well discovered, the man who knows all cleans the slate of our sin and casts vision for a new life, a life of joy and freedom unspeakable. Only the God who is our Father and only the God of whom it is said *who art in heaven* can provide the amazing act of *grace*. It all starts with *I found a man . . . !*

Man's search for God has taken on many shapes and sizes. The complexities of the search have found definition culturally throughout history. Many forms and methods are well documented; gods worthy of unlimited imagination have been sought. The image of sundry gods has been captured in art while others have been blindly worshiped through loud incantations, some even through the sacrificing of infants. Most inquiries and searches for God seem to be tainted by the lack of genuine worship—the standards by which our moral and ethical conduct is affirmed. They all seem to question, "Is there reward in exchange for my loyal allegiance?" Obviously, this distortion has even found way into the Christian faith.

The *what's in it for me* mindset distorts the essence of genuine faith. God promises fellowship with him. Hope is never compromised or forfeited even when despair or pain, perhaps even death, claim momentary victory over our frailness. But the faith we so desperately need is assured by knowing the presence of him who loves us and is the *otherness* we must have. The search by so many has been overthought and misguided. The coming of Jesus into history answers the question with simplicity and exactness. Read again the story of the Samaritan women. It tells it all. To know God is a journey. I absolutely love the Greek parsing of the word *saved*. What Paul wanted to remind was that we are saved; the punctiliar moment has happened. However, the language must also be understood to teach that salvation is an ongoing process during which we are being made into his image and, in the end, salvation will be complete (Eph 2:8).

I remember the ongoing struggle I went through before publicly and personally acknowledging my need for salvation. It seemed defined by two immutable crossroads. On one hand, I passionately sought to be loved in the most profound of ways. I needed to be loved and accepted for who I was. I needed the kind of affirmation that transcended my weaknesses and my journey to self-destruction. On the other hand, there was a lingering hunger for a way of life that was beyond my sinful nature. A part of who I understood myself to be could not be glossed over or be eliminated by some *do good and you will be fine* feeling, an emotion that jockeyed for preeminence in my world of rationalization. I knew, regardless of a favorable and attractive way of doing life, that I was incomplete, lost in a world of inconsistency and often despair. I also recognized that lostness was not kindly exempt without a confession of my inability to manage the drudgery and misdirection in life to which I was enslaved.

How large is this miracle called salvation? I have just provided the consummate example of the interrobang. Please look at it carefully. The mystery of knowing God by fully realizing that the phrase is the exclamatory and not the interrogative can be the answer. Salvation is a miracle made possible by the God who loves you, who is also the God of all creation. By His Grace you are being saved, both now and forever more. Amen!

Conclusion

Additional Reflections

IF YOU HAVE READ this book through and are now at its conclusion, thank you for hanging in there with me. Clearly this book is biographical in nature, and to a large extent, is the retelling of my personal story and the recounting of my journey in faith. If you have stuck with it to this point, you have been exposed to my journey; you know how I have moved from possessing a low sense of self-worth to my understanding of just how much God loves me, so much so that in Christ I have been forgiven and can joyfully hold onto the redemption extended to me.

More than making this story about my struggles, my accomplishments, my hurts, or my shame, I have attempted to tell of God's good work in me. Through a dependency on Holy Scripture, I have not only shared my story, but have also attempted to acknowledge my need for on-going redemption. Even with our flawed and sinful natures, God walks with us through our times in the desert. It is his story of redemption that shines a light on where we have fallen as he invites our conviction and confession of sin—sins not only that we have committed, but the mistakes, unjust actions, and mis-directions to which we will, in the future, succumb.

Perhaps you are now, or have been in the past, in Christian service. Maybe you are just starting out, excited about what lies ahead. Maybe you have found yourself walking through fire and are now unsure of how to navigate from where you find yourself. You may be overwhelmed. You may have fallen short of what you believe to have been God's call on your life. Maybe you committed some sin that hurt you and/or others or made some misguided choices that tarnished your Christian witness. Maybe you have found it necessary to walk away from a ministry in which you were sure

God wanted you. You may be filled with guilt and shame for being unfaithful to God's call on your life. The questions run endlessly.

Like me, you may have suffered the loss of his *giftedness* and mourn that loss. You may be at the point of searching to find a new place of service using other gifts he has given you. Whatever it was that brought you to the place of reading this book, I hope that you have found a few nuggets of truth with which you can either identify or from which you can find hope. Maybe a *revisit* will now surface. Who knows? Perhaps, even in reading this book, you have found a place from which to launch your search to return to Bethel.

I encourage you to take a prayerful look back to those parts of the book that struck an emotional or even spiritual chord with you. It is my prayer that you will find inspiration in a closer look at God's work in and through my story. I challenge you to prayerfully seek him in all things as your story is being written.

Bibliography

Alport, Gordon. *The Individual and His Religion*. New York: McMillion, 1950.
Banton, Roland. *Here I Stand: A Life of Martin Luther*. Nashville: Abington, 1950.
Brunner, Emil. *Eternal Hope*. Cambridge: Lutterworth, 1954.
Burns, Robert. *Tam O'Shanter*. Chicago: The Poetry Foundation, 2022.
Buttrick, George. *The Parables of Jesus*. Baker: Grand Rapids, 1928.
Camus, Albert. *The Stranger*. Translated by Stuart Gilbert. New York: Albert A. Knopf, 1946.
Claypool, John. *Tracks of a Fellow Struggler*. Harrisburg: Morehouse, 2004.
de Cervantess, Miguel. *Don Quixote*. Edited and Translated by John Rutherford. New York: Random House, 2005.
Eastman, Carol. *Five Easy Pieces*. Directed by Rob Rafelson. BBS Productions, 1970.
Elliot, Elizabeth. *Through Gates of Splendor*. New York: Harper & Row, 1957.
Fisher, J. *The New Covenant*. Youth Musical. Waco: Light Records, 1975.
Fudge, Edward William. *The Fire that Consumes*. New York: Verdict, 1982.
Hemingway, Ernest. *A Farewell to Arms,* New York: Scribner, 1929.
Houston, Keith. "The Interrobang." https://shadycharacters.co.uk/series/the-interrobang/.
Ivins, Edward Gordon. *This Way Out*. Helena: Avondale, 1925.
Jeremias, Joachim. *The Lord's Prayer*. Translated by John Henry Paul Reuman, Vol 8. Cambridge: Facet Books, 1964.
King, Martin Luther. *The Autobiography of Martin Luther King Jr*. Edited by Clayborne Carson. New York: Warner, 1998.
Lindsay, Hal. *The Late Great Planet Earth*. Grand Rapids: Zondervan, 1970.
McLuhan, M. *Understanding Media: The Extensions of Man*. Canada: McGraw Hill, 1964.
Neider, Charles. *The Autobiography of Mark Twain*. Harper: New York, 2000.
Parker, Alan, dir. *Five Easy Pieces*. Orion Pictures, 1988.
Rafelson, R., dir. *Mississippi Burning*. Columbia Pictures, 1970.
Sartre, Jean Paul, "No Exit." In *No Exit, and Three Other Plays*, translated by Stewart Gilbert, 1–24. New York: Vintage International, 1989.
Schwartz, David A. "Watchmaker Analogy: A Self-Refuting Argument." *Huffpost*, October 10, 2012. https://www.huffpost.com/entry/intelligent-design-watchmaker_b_1730878.
Scofield, Cyrus I. *The Scofield Reference Bible*. Oxford: Oxford University Press, 1922.
Severns, Maggie, et al. "They All Got Careless: How Falwell Kept His Grip on Liberty Amid Sexual 'Games.'" *Politico*, November 1, 2020. https://news.yahoo.com/falwell-kept-grip-liberty-amid-115206368.html.

BIBLIOGRAPHY

Shakespere, William. *The Complete Works of William Shakespeare.* New York: Gramercy, 1990.
Tennyson, Alfred Lord. "Tithonus." https://poets.org/poem/tithonus.
Thielicke, Helmet. *Life Can Begin Again.* Translated by John W. Doberstein. Cambridge: The Lutterworth, 2016.
Toynbee, Arnold. *A Study of History.* 12 vols. Oxford: Oxford University Press, 1934–61.
Wasserman, Dale. *Man of La Mancha.* Goodspeed Opera House, East Hammam, CT.

www.ingramcontent.com/pod-product-compliance
Lightning Source LLC
Chambersburg PA
CBHW072135160426
43197CB00012B/2111